I0153450

LOVING OSCAR

Yolanda Lopez

Azalea Art Press
Sonoma | CA

© Yolanda Lopez | 2019.
All Rights Reserved.

ISBN: 978-1-943471-39-3

Cover Photo | Connie and Oscar Lopez
Cover Design | Linda Lopez

For all my brothers and sisters
with love

CONTENTS

Powerlessness and silence
go together.

— *Margaret Atwood*

INTRODUCTION

Memoir builds on our truths
so that others can shelter there.

This is my mother's story. Sharing it with family members has been on my mind for the last ten years.

Consuelo (Connie) Maria Lopez came of age in a time of war and great changes. Her relationship to her family, her husband, and her children defined her life. An intelligent, loyal, religious woman, she lived in the shadow of strong personalities. Her background and upbringing discouraged her from speaking out.

Loving Oscar is my attempt to make my mother's voice heard.

In the beginning it was difficult to explain why I was writing my mother's story. Some family members thought the past should be laid to rest. However, it felt important to pursue the truths of her life. My siblings and I never knew the audacious young woman who had so many hopes for her future. We only knew a mother who was beaten down by the circumstances pressing upon her.

When my father divorced my mother, she was left with six young children to raise. He later remarried and had six children with his second wife. These two families would grow up in very different circumstances and with little interaction; therefore, much of this story is unknown to some family members. Some information may be shocking, but it reflects the times the incidents occurred. There is no intent to malign anyone, only to explain why they acted as they did—which was often with good but misguided intentions.

Many details in the story were relayed to me and other siblings directly by my mother and father. Some of the dialogue and events are recreated though accounts of her children and through research of original documents as well as DNA testing of children in the first family to verify my father's bloodline.

The funny thing about writing a book about your mother is that you learn a lot about yourself. It led me to consider my role as a daughter. Had I judged my mother too harshly while growing up? Instead of appreciating my mother, I spent years withdrawing from her. I had been unaware of the heavy burdens she endured, but I now understand what an astounding job she did with the little she had. Now it is too late to tell her, but I hope my mother knows what is in my heart.

This book has led me to a much clearer understanding of how choices can change the course of individual destinies and bring us both excruciating pain and great joy. My mother's choices changed her path and that of my brothers and sisters. They definitely changed my life.

Like all stories there is always more. We know the end of my mother's story too well, but it is my hope that we will also understand the beginning and the middle of our parents' relationship.

This book is my mother's legacy to her children and is imparted with love and affection by her eldest daughter.

— Yolanda Lopez, 2019

PREFACE

It was a time of reflection, but also a time for revelations.

It was a dazzling, sunny, yet very sad day for the family of Connie Lopez that Friday, May 27, 2016. All six of Connie's children attended the memorial service in the Julia Morgan Chapel in Piedmont, California, just a short distance from where Connie had lived for thirty years.

At the Chapel of Chimes, the time had come to say goodbye to their beloved mother and each came with their own thoughts and memories. Music expressly created by Rosa, Connie's youngest daughter, played softly in the background. As mourners entered the chapel, Connie's favorite song, *Ave Maria* could be heard echoing throughout the chamber. Pictures of Connie and her children flashed across the television monitor.

Several children spoke at the podium, sharing their feelings about their mother, whom they called "Chula." Daniel, her second son spoke last. His tender eulogy summed up Connie's love for her children. Hesitating and then pausing before commencing, he said:

I am not sure I wanted to address this today, but I'll say it, anyway. There was a huge lack of hugs and kisses when we were growing up. It wasn't until I met my wonderful wife and her beautiful little girls that I realized how important affection is to the development of a young child. That is also when I realized how much I had missed as a young boy growing up, so I have a good idea of how deeply it has touched each of you.

I believe the true measure of a person is what is in their heart, whether there is empathy and compassion for other people. I would like to tell you a story about the "heart" of our mom.

As some of you know, Mom received a small amount of money from her mother when she died in 1978. The money she received could be used to supplement her tiny pension from J. J. Newberry. It was a chance to improve the quality of her life. When she told me she wanted to invest it for her children, we got into a huge argument, but she would not budge. So, I figured Mom was thinking long term in case she needed money in her later years, so she wouldn't have to burden her children. She was always fiercely independent about money. So, mom did without things for decades as her account grew to three times the original amount.

When Mom turned ninety, she called me and told me to set up an account to be shared equally among her children when she passed away. She said this to me as though I was a disinterested third party. Chafing a bit, I said, "Last time I checked I was still one of your children." She laughed and said, "You know what I mean." I said it was a bad idea because everyone in the family knew she would outlive us all. She didn't laugh and said, "Just get it done." So, I made it happen. When Mom called four years ago, her plan finally dawned on me. The money received from her mother so long ago was never meant for her. It was always earmarked for her children. That was her long-range plan.

You see, Mom wanted us to have a gift from her when she was gone, a gift that would make a difference in our lives. So, I ask you today, are these the actions of a *mom who was not thinking about her children? Does it sound like the actions of a mom who was not concerned about the well-being of her sons and daughters? Are these the actions of a mom who did not love her children? Of course not, these are the actions of a thoughtful, caring mom who just didn't know how to express herself emotionally. But she found a way, didn't she? And it came straight from her heart.*

So, I want you to do me a personal favor. When you receive your gift and you purchase something for yourself or your family, on that day, I want you to think of our mom giving you hugs and kisses that you never received. That is mom's way of telling you how important you are to her. That is our mom loving you. If we all do this, we will not only be better people for it, but we'll put a huge smile on mom's face because she'll know that we all understood.

Several family members wiped tears from their eyes while the music faded in the background. All six children exited the Julia Morgan Chapel, walking down the hall for a luncheon held in Connie's honor. The questions for each were: Had they known their mother? Had they understood what she had given up for them? And, more importantly, did they know how loved they were? So many sacrifices had been made. Had it been worth it for her? Shaking off these gloomy thoughts, most of the children elected to remember the happy times as they toasted their mother one last time.

Connie's eldest daughter, Yolanda, trailed behind the rest of the family with her own thoughts and regrets regarding her mother's life. She worried that despite having survived the difficult years and raising six kids, her mother's life had not included enough joy and surely not enough love. Had her father ever loved her mother? Her earliest recollections of her parents' relationship was rocky as far back as she could remember. Had her mother loved their father? For the greater part of her life, Connie had only spoken with bitterness when discussing Oscar. Her words were "Your father..." and then she would trail off. Was there love in the beginning?

But Yolanda knew something that the others did not. Many years later, long after his divorce from her mother and well into his marriage to his second wife, Julia, Oscar had made a special trip to Northern California to talk about the early days of his marriage to Connie.

On that visit, Oscar confessed. He told Yolanda:

"I made a lot of mistakes, and am here to ask your forgiveness for all the things that happened to my first family. However, you need to know the entire story now.

Your mom painted me as the bad guy her entire life. She told you and your brothers and sisters I had hurt her, harmed the family with secrets and my relationship with Julia, and finally for leaving you kids when your mom was pregnant with your youngest sister. Well, I did do a lot of terrible things, but I want you to know the entire story.

You need to know how it started and understand we both made some serious mistakes. I am not saying mine were not worse, just that there are lots of things you kids never knew. I have always loved all my children, but was torn between loyalty to both families."

Connie never knew her eldest daughter had heard "the rest of the story" and Yolanda never revealed to her mother what her dad had told her that fateful day. These revelations would change Yolanda's understanding of her mother and father's relationship and lead to a greater appreciation of the complexities that made up Connie's life as well as how she had suffered for some of her early choices. It also helped her to understand Connie's bitterness toward Oscar.

Her father's confession gave her information that made her pause. She realized how Connie had loved her children and how hurtful some of Connie's family's actions had been to her over the years, even though they continued to help in times of need.

What follows is Connie's story.

LOVING
OSCAR

Connie Lopez

CHAPTER 1

Connie gathered the dark blue sweater around her slim shoulders as she glimpsed out of the open storefront window. Slivers of sunlight filtered through the gray clouds darkening the sky. The scent of rain lingered in the air hinting of an upcoming storm.

Turning back, Connie glanced around the grocery store at the customers milling about. Patrons picked up items, checked the price, and then replaced them to their original place. Others grabbed their selected groceries, scurrying towards the large cash register positioned at the front of the market. Money was a scarce commodity for the folks shopping at this 12th and Temple Street neighborhood grocery store on this late dreary afternoon in January 1942.

Connie's parents owned the store. The children, along with both parents, were required to assist with the day-to-day operations. Situated in an impoverished area of Los Angeles, the store carried a limited supply of groceries. Mexican and Jewish store patrons frequented this local community market for last minute shopping on their way home from work and errands. Fresh fruit sat lined up in wooden crates next to the shiny green jalapenos, habaneros and Fresno chilies. Bunches of limp cilantros leaned sideways in empty jam jars filled with water. Boxes of matzo crackers, along with glass jars of gefilte fish and packaged rugelach lined the shelves. Braided challah lay next to loaves of Wonder Bread. The market sold a limited supply of beer and wine.

Connie was on duty today. Stacks of newspapers were piled high at the store's entrance. Patrons could not avoid seeing the headline: NEW WEST COAST RAIDS FEARED blazed across the front page of the *Daily Los Angeles Herald.*

Listless and distracted, Connie was worried. Her mother was threatening to take the entire family back to Mexico. Connie did not even know where that would be. She did not want to know. She wanted to stay in the United States. Born in San Antonio, Texas, Connie could only remember Los Angeles as her home. Her mother, Maria, repeatedly declared that she would not let her three sons serve in the army or in any of the Armed Forces; therefore, she was taking them back to Mexico. Tony, the youngest son, was in no immediate danger because of his age. The boys did not respond to their mother's tirades. They remained silent as her mother's warnings broke the peace at the dinner table.

Connie wanted to talk to her two older sisters about what they could do to stay in the U. S., but she was afraid to bring the matter up. Her sisters had shown little concern about leaving the country. Each time their mother, deliberated about exiting the country, the elder girls acted bored, so Connie had no inkling as to their thoughts about the imminent move. As the youngest daughter, Connie had been the favorite child from her earliest days. This made her reluctant to bring this subject up to her older sisters, who treated her with disdain. Talking to Ruth, her sister closest to her in age, was of no use either. She knew that Ruthie would shrug away Connie's worries with a noncommittal response.

Connie needed a plan to stay. At twenty years old, her life had just started. Outraged that her parents would drag her out of the country to a place in Mexico she had never been or seen frightened her, particularly since her grasp of the Spanish language was not that strong. *No, I want to stay in L.A. I will stay in L.A.,* she thought stubbornly to herself.

CHAPTER 2

Maria was strict with her children, compelling them to adhere to her established rules. According to family lore, Maria had been forced into an arranged marriage to an older man at age fifteen. Connie and her siblings believed this story that had been passed on to the family as an accurate portrayal of her mother's difficult beginning. Yet, when checked many years later, the official records revealed a different account. In fact, immigration archives disclosed that Maria and her husband, Florencio, entered the United States at Laredo, Texas "by foot" on July 26, 1916, with three children—Lucille and twin boys, Florencio (known as Alfred) and Frank.

The paperwork disclosed that Florencio was a laborer/carpenter, 36 years of age, from San Luis Potosi, Mexico, his birthplace. It listed his wife's name as Jesus Gallardo. She would later be known as Maria in her legal documents. Maria was 27 years old when she crossed into the U.S. and originally from Villa Arriaga, a small locality in the greater San Luis Potosi district. Florencio and Maria had married in Torreon, Mexico, on February 15, 1908, when Maria was 19 years old.

Raised in rural Mexico, Maria held on to the notion that female children remained at home with their parents until they married. To do anything less was scandalous and not permitted. She had told her four girls they could not stay in the United States unmarried and unchaperoned. Not only that—Maria did not believe in dating. That was only for gringos. It was not allowed in Maria's household. The sisters, who all lived at home, often snuck out under some pretense or other to see young suitors. All were old enough—Lucille was 34, Carmen was 24, and Ruth was 22. Connie was the youngest and had not dated.

Maria staunchly believed you could only trust your family. Friends were something you kept at a distance. Family was family, and it required you to stick together and support each other. She did not encourage outside friendships or relationships for herself or for her children. Maria had acquaintances she did business with and others she saw at church, but not ones who came over to her house or ones with whom she shared intimate information. Connie and her brothers and sisters would integrate this belief system into their lives, never conscious of its legacy.

CHAPTER 3

Lost in thought, Connie wished she had someone she could talk to about her situation. Just then, the store's doorbell rang announcing a new customer. She turned and saw it was a one of their regulars, a handsome frequent customer. Oscar was over six feet tall with broad shoulders, dark brooding eyes, wavy jet-black hair, and movie star good looks.

Oscar's gait conveyed the appearance of a tough guy. Connie was not sure how old he was, but guessed somewhere in his mid-twenties. Yet, he had a lost look about him, which is perhaps why Maria and her husband were fond of him. Oscar knew her mom and dad well. She knew her mother felt sorry for him because he seemed so alone.

Connie guessed he lived nearby because of his routine visits. He glanced around the store as though he was looking for someone. Connie knew he fancied one of her older sisters—Carmen—who had green eyes and beautiful golden blond hair. Carmen was not in the store today. Distractedly, Oscar asked for her mom. Connie explained that her mother was not around this afternoon and without paying any attention to her, the young man put his money on the counter and made his way out of the store.

Although Connie did not have Carmen's striking looks, she was pretty in her own way, with large brown eyes and shiny brown hair. Despite this, she knew a secret.

Carmen had a boyfriend with whom she was madly in love and whom she planned to marry. She wished she had a boyfriend, too. Dreamily, she thought, if only Oscar could be her boyfriend. But the dashing, dark-haired customer barely noticed her when he came in. Even she had to admit she was no match in the beauty department when compared to her older sisters, Carmen and Lucille.

Protective of all the girls, her family trusted that no daughter would dare leave the family unit until safely married. Still, Connie fantasized about what it would feel like to be romantically involved with a man, something she had not yet experienced, especially not with someone as striking as Oscar. Shy, and the youngest of six, with limited exposure to men other than her brothers, Connie was sheltered from the realities of everyday life.

CHAPTER 4

At dinner that night, her mother reiterated that they would leave for Mexico soon. Frightened by the prospect, Connie knew she had to act quickly if she wished to stay. Her thoughts returned to Oscar when an unlikely idea imbedded itself in her head. Perhaps, if Connie could convince him to marry her, she would not have to go. It was true that Oscar did not appear enthralled with her nor had she been on a date with anyone, much less someone like him. Oscar seemed so more experienced and worldlier than Connie. But a girl could hope . . .

Later, in bed, Connie resolved to get the courage to talk to Oscar. It would be awkward, but she had to do it if she wanted to stay. *But what can I say to Oscar that will convince him and that will keep him from thinking I am not stark raving mad?* For the next couple of days, she kept running different ideas through her head. Oscar had not shown up on any of the days she managed the store, giving Connie more time to formulate her plan. She did not feel fully prepared to confront him with her proposition. *Darn,* she thought to herself, *I am not even sure how to bring up the subject. It will be embarrassing. Will I even be able to get the words out? What should I say? What would be most persuasive?*

More than a week and a half had elapsed before Connie saw Oscar again. Holding a bottle of milk and two beers in both hands, Oscar moved to the register where Connie stood ringing up the last customer. Biting her lips nervously, Connie asked him how he was doing. Surprised by the question, Oscar mumbled, "Fine." Studying Oscar, Connie whispered, "I have a question to ask you, if you have a minute." *Stop hesitating*, she scolded herself. *Have gumption. Ask him! Hurry. Ask him!*

Oscar focused his full attention on Connie. For a minute, she could not speak. Gathering every ounce of courage she could muster, she blurted out, "My mother is taking us back to Mexico and I don't want to go. I need a reason to stay. I was wondering if you would marry me?"

Oscar's face revealed his astonishment and confusion. Without a moment's hesitation to her startling proposal, he countered, "I don't even know you. Why would I marry you? Are you crazy? We've never even been out on a date."

Flustered, but swiftly recovering, Connie replied, "Well, maybe we could go to movies sometimes...you know, to get to know each other."

Chiding herself, she wondered how she could have uttered such a stupid response. Shaking his head to the girl's tepid suggestion, he stated, "No, I am not marrying anyone. I've got my papers shipping me overseas and I'm waiting for my final orders." Grabbing his groceries, he bolted out of the store without a backward glance.

Tears filled Connie's eyes. How could she have blown her chance? Perhaps if Oscar knew her better or if she could explain how frantic she was to stay; she could convince him to help her. For the next couple of days, she kept an eye out for Oscar, but he did not return to the store.

To make matters worse, there was no one Connie could talk to about what she had done and what she had hoped would happen. She sent a quick prayer to her favorite saint asking for help in changing Oscar's mind, but then it occurred to Connie that she might just like him more than she thought. She could get hurt. Connie dismissed such thoughts since he did not even appear to like her. Mulling it over in her head, she decided she would do whatever was necessary to make that happen, no matter how humiliating or hard. Connie was not a courageous girl, but she would have to be if she wanted to stay in Los Angeles.

A few days later, she bumped into Oscar entering the store as she was leaving. Connie abruptly stopped in front of him staring deep into his dark eyes. Without further thought and before she lost her nerve, Connie asked Oscar if he would like to go to the movies with her. Surprised, Oscar seemed about to say no when Connie said, "Please, please, give me a chance."

Distressed, the young man looked about as though searching for a way out, then abruptly acquiesced. "Just the movies, no marriage," Oscar declared as he moved away quickly.

They agreed to meet two days later at the theater. Oscar was unsure why he agreed to the date with Connie. He was not interested in her, and he was not getting married. *Hell, I am shipping out any day now and marriage is the last thing I need to worry about.* And then, too, there was that commitment he made to his childhood sweetheart, Julia, long ago.

Though uneasy, Connie surreptitiously glanced sideways at Oscar as they entered the theater. Connie loved going to the movies with her sisters and friends, but today she was too nervous and unsure of what her next move should be to concentrate on the film. Wanting to raise the subject of marriage, but fearing it would spoil the evening, she said nothing. She was trying so hard to make a good impression.

On their way home, Connie risked asking him again if he would marry her. This time she disclosed he would be doing her a big favor and it would allow her to stay in California. Bewildered, Oscar stared at Connie, astounded that she would not drop the subject and that she had the nerve to bring it up again. Oscar did not know how determined Connie was to stay.

Oscar retorted roughly, "I told you I don't want to get married. I am leaving soon."

"Please, will you at least consider it?" she begged, hating the whiny tone in her voice.

A look of pure annoyance crossed Oscar's face as he walked away without a further word.

CHAPTER 5

Days sped by with no sign of Oscar. Connie agonized that he had already shipped out and that she had lost her one opportunity to remain in Los Angeles. Oscar showed up at the market on the fifth day and asked if he could speak to her privately. Talking in a low whisper, Connie's reluctant suitor confessed he felt sorry for her situation. Oscar confided he knew her mother's temperament well enough to know that the matriarch would follow through with her plans to leave the country. Because of this, and despite his better judgment, Oscar advised a thunderstruck Connie that he would—albeit grudgingly—agree to marry her, but they had to do it soon because he had gotten his final papers to ship out.

And so, they decided they would marry. Oscar proposed they meet at the county courthouse to marry in two days' time. Though plagued with serious doubts about the whole business of marriage, Oscar felt compelled to help Connie. He himself was unsure why.

Overjoyed and overcome with relief, Connie kept singing to herself, *I do not have to leave. I do not have to leave.* She wanted to tell everyone yet could tell no one. She could not jeopardize the marriage by having anyone know. It would have to be a secret. The newly-affianced Connie did not think she could even tell her fiancé that no one could know she was getting married. Despite the need for secrecy, the bride-to-be was ecstatic as she offered a special prayer of thanks in gratitude for her reprieve.

Connie's thoughts turned to the immediate worry of what to wear to her wedding. She had to call in sick from work for half a day if she was to make it to the county courthouse by 10:00 AM, and Oscar had mentioned something about meeting later that evening for dinner to celebrate. The thought occurred to her he might expect more, too, but just fleetingly; she could only worry about one thing at a time. Connie wished she had someone talk to so she could share her wonderful news, but there was no one. Thus, she held her secret securely in her heart.

As agreed, the young couple met on the steps of the courthouse and walked in together. While the groom had dressed casually, the bride had taken unusual care to look her best, as this was her wedding day. Wearing a stylish narrow collared light blue suit that fit her well, Connie felt elegant and ready for her special day. It bothered her a little she did not have a white gown or at least a white suit, but Connie let go of those thoughts as she said her "I do." The ceremony was quick, with the court clerks serving as witnesses. Oscar gave Connie a swift peck on the cheek, and she was a married woman.

On the way out, Oscar said, "We'll meet at 7:00 PM at 7th & Broadway tonight."

Nodding yes, Connie made her way to work wondering what she would say to get out of the house that night. Even more frightening, no one had prepared her for marital sex. Connie had limited knowledge of how it worked. Sex was not something she could ask her mother about and Connie was too shy to ask her sisters. Not to mention, they would be suspicious why their little sister was asking such intimate questions. *I will have to wing it and figure out what to do,* she thought to herself. *I think I can do that. I hope I can do that. I wish I knew more about it.*

Walking home that evening, Oscar decided he needed to be dressed appropriately for his wedding night. He needed a suit for dinner and the "after" event. Oscar owned no suit, but the uncle he lived with did. Oscar asked to borrow the suit which triggered Uncle Joe's curiosity.

"Why," he asked his nephew, "would you need to borrow my old-fashioned suit?" Oscar offered no explanation, shrugging. He did not want to tell the uncle he had gotten married. He was in no mood to hear a bunch of crap about why he would go do something like that when he was leaving.

The suit was too large, a strange shade of grey, and out-of-date, but it was the best he could do at the last minute. Once shaved, Oscar slipped into his borrowed suit and made his way to their agreed meeting place. The young groom thought himself rather handsome.

It was a balmy Los Angeles evening as Oscar stood on the corner of 7th & Broadway waiting for his bride. He was a little early, but that was okay. Oscar eyed the people rushing up and down the street on their way home and out to dinner. His nervousness surprised him. He had booked a room in the hotel he was standing in front of waiting for Connie. First, they had dinner reservations at 7:00 PM at a fancy Italian restaurant down the street, one a friend had recommended. These arrangements had taken the last bit of his money, but it was his wedding night and he only had a couple days left in Los Angeles, so why not celebrate? Oscar had to admit he was a little excited and somewhat curious. Connie and he had never even shared a real kiss.

By 7:15 PM, there was no sign of Connie, and Oscar was growing angry. By 8:30 PM, he was furious and regretting trying to help her. Waiting until 10:00 PM before heading home, a seething Oscar promised himself he would have the marriage annulled as soon as possible. He had wasted money on a room and had primped for nothing. He wondered if she had ever planned on showing up or if it all had just been a ruse to get herself married.

Dressed and ready to go, Connie kept watching the clock as it inched closer to their scheduled meeting time. Her brother Tony had been ill for days and his condition had worsened in the early afternoon. Maria, in answer to the call of maternal intuition, wanted to take him to the hospital that evening and needed Connie to accompany her on the bus, as Maria's English was limited. Connie tried to protest, but she had no choice but to go with her mother.

With no way to reach Oscar, she did not know what to do. Connie knew he would be angry, but secretly she was somewhat relieved since she was not sure she was ready for the rest of the "stuff" matrimony entailed. She hoped Oscar would come into the store the next day, so she could explain why she had not shown up. She needed her new husband to understand she had intended to meet him.

Returning from the hospital after midnight, Connie headed straight for her bed. Torn with guilt about not meeting Oscar, she tossed and turned as she tried to fall asleep. It was supposed to be her wedding night. *Please,* she told herself, *let it go.* But her mind kept reeling, reminding her he had done her a huge favor and she had failed to repay it by failing to show on their wedding night. Surely, he would be angry. She would have been.

The following day, October 10, 1942, newspapers buzzed with reports that large groups of servicemen were being shipped out of Grand Central Railroad Station that afternoon. Connie missed work again to see if Oscar was one of the soldiers being dispatched to Europe. It was vital she spoke with him before he left. Connie did not know if he would be in the group leaving, but she recalled Oscar telling her he had been waiting for his final leave notice.

Dashing off the bus, Connie could see long lines of soldiers waiting in front of the station. Hordes of people and soldiers gathered in clusters outside and inside the cavernous building. The crowded, noisy station was intimidating. Suddenly overwhelmed, Connie wondered how she would ever find Oscar in this staggering throng of soldiers. Everywhere she turned there were groups of soldiers talking and jostling each other, family members crying, while others were fervently kissing and hugging.

Connie heard her name being called and turned to see Oscar waving at her. He did not seem happy to see her. In fact, he appeared angry. Worried about a confrontation, Connie rushed up to him halting in front of him. Oscar's acerbic comment was not unexpected.

"Well, I guess you showed up now even if it is after the wedding evening. Connie, why did you leave me standing there for hours with no word? Never mind, I don't care what the reason was. It doesn't make a difference. It was a terrible mistake to marry you. I plan on getting an annulment once I arrive overseas."

Connie attempted to explain about her brother being sick and her mother insisting she accompany her to the hospital. Oscar did not believe her. Incredibly, her new husband appeared settled on the notion she had tricked him into a "paper" marriage, which was not true. Connie intended to meet her husband at 7th & Broadway at 7:00 PM. She had a damn good reason for not showing up. *How can I make him believe me?* she wondered as the line started moving.

"Please slow down, Oscar," she whispered to him, as the line progressed.

Still ranting as the line of soldiers inched forward, Oscar tersely instructed Connie to write him and said they would get it all sorted out when he reached his first overseas location. Soldiers elbowed each other as they glanced at the young couple. The line sped up and even though Connie hastened her steps, she could not keep up.

Then Oscar disappeared into the line boarding the train. He did not even look back. Connie did not know what to think. She had hoped to convince Oscar that she had not intended to deceive him.

What could I have done differently, she asked herself as she wrung her hands and watched the long line of soldiers completely disappear into the train. As it edged forward, the train spat out puffs of steam as it gathered speed. Tearful and unsure, Connie stayed glued to her spot looking at the train until it was no longer visible before turning away and heading to work. Tears slid down her cheeks, but she brushed them away as she ran to catch her bus.

CHAPTER 6

Oscar shipped out that day. Upon reaching his first destination in Italy, they asked him to provide personal information on his marital status. "Married, I guess," he said, "but I am getting an annulment as soon as I can do the paperwork." Notwithstanding, the Army required Oscar to provide his wife's name as she was entitled to receive part of her husband's compensation while overseas. This information only incensed Oscar more.

Oscar's first letter to Connie was an angry one, recounting the hardships he was enduring overseas and bitterly raving about what had happened between them. Connie wrote Oscar back requesting that he not send letters to her addressed as "Mrs. Oscar Lopez" as no one knew they married. She could not tell her family.

"Please," she begged in her letter, "Send nothing in that name, only my maiden name."

Receiving this new information further exasperated Oscar. He could not understand why the marriage had to remain secret. Distraught, Oscar decided he would no longer write letters to his wife while away. Nor did Connie attempt to write her husband again while he was overseas. She wanted to write him but did not know what she could say to make it right. Discouraged, she decided it would be best to wait until he returned so she could explain to him again face-to-face what had happened. Connie did not like conflict.

Connie agonized over Oscar's whereabouts and hoped he would make it back despite the continual reports of the growing number of war casualties from overseas. Connie did not know the dangers Oscar faced daily. In fact, she did not know where he was stationed overseas. She prayed every night that he be kept safe from harm and injury.

As with many ironies in life, one of the main reasons Oscar had consented to "the marriage" was so he would have someone to write to and share his thoughts and fears while abroad. He had no one who would write to him. Oscar longed for the closeness of family, something he never had as a child. A wife, he thought, would serve that role, but that was not to be. Connie's silence only reinforced his worst beliefs about their tenuous relationship.

Oscar already had a deep well of anger within him because of his tumultuous childhood. His brief and unsatisfactory matrimony experience reinforced his distrust. It made him miserable and angry at himself for having gotten into such a mess.

Private Lopez was stationed at some of the most dangerous zones during the war—Sicily, Northern Africa, the Rhineland, and Northern France. Through luck or providence, he was never injured despite fighting in some of the worst World War II battles, with one "minor" exception. While in Africa in the fall of 1942, Oscar contracted yellow fever (also known as malaria) resulting in placement on inactive service from October 1942 through early November 1942 for recuperation.

On June 6, 1944, Oscar found himself in Normandy. The Normandy invasion began with overnight parachutes, glider landings, and massive air attacks. In the cold, early morning hours, the troops from the United States landed on Omaha and Utah beaches and slowly marched up the shoreline. When he spoke of that momentous day, Oscar painted a picture of hellish chaos. He recounted bombs falling all around him as he and his comrades made their way up the beach. He recounted how he dove into a ditch filled with excrement to avoid being shot. Private Oscar Lopez lived; other buddies were not so lucky.

Even decades later, Oscar seldom recounted details of the war years except for his experiences with the Italians in Sicily. He spoke of them and their generosity during those challenging times with great awe. Though very poor, the Sicilians graciously shared the little food they had with the GIs stationed near their homes. As he recalled, they had no plates or silverware. Their hosts poured cooked spaghetti onto the middle of the table and then poured the sauce on top for all to eat with their hands. Oscar said those were some of the most touching and memorable meals of his life.

CHAPTER 7

The Army shipped Oscar back to the States on December 23, 1944 and stationed him at Camp Haan Army Base in Riverside, California. Prior to the start of World War II, in November 1940, the United States Army began construction of a sizeable Coast Artillery Antiaircraft Replacement Training Center after it was determined a coastal base was needed next to the army airfield. Later renamed Marsh Air Reserve Base, it opened in 1941 and served as an important part of the World War II antiaircraft strategy used for training and deployment.

At one time, the base housed up to 80,000 soldiers, covered 8,000 acres, with 353 wooden buildings and 2,549 tents comprised of hospital, chapels, exchanges, sewers, and mess halls. Buildings and living quarters were rudimentary, often constructed from 14 x 14 plywood sheets, with no insulation, finishing, or paint. The plywood sheets were the only means of protection the soldiers had from the elements. Most barracks contained a wooden floor, a potbelly stove, and canvas cots with three-inch mattresses. They assigned six men to each building. Space was limited. Necessity being the mother of invention, the soldiers' duffel bags often led double lives as their bureaus.

Soldiers stationed at Camp Haan were assigned to the 815 Antiaircraft Artillery (AAA) Automatic Weapons (AW) Battalion. The Army's AAA weapon of choice was the 40 mm automatic gun M1. GIs spent hours learning how to operate and maintain their guns. Private Lopez received gun training there and certified as an Expert Light Machine Gun operator in January 1943 and later as a Marksman Rifle MI in February 1944.

The City of San Bernardino was near the Army base and in 1944 had the dubious national reputation of being a "City of Vice." Soldiers were expressly barred from the city's prostitution district during their stay at the camp. Military police patrolled the streets where the brothels operated to ensure soldiers stayed within allowed boundaries. Private Lopez was assigned to work as a military policeman while stationed in Camp Haan, a role he continued to serve in until his honorable discharge on October 10, 1945. Oscar was decorated with three Overseas Service Bars, and he received the European, African Mideastern Campaign medal for his service.

CHAPTER 8

Upon returning to the States in late December 1944, Oscar was granted a short leave early in January 1945. He took a Greyhound bus from Riverside to his hometown of Tucson, Arizona to visit his sisters and brothers. They were all living with various family members.

His mother was 27 years old when Oscar was born in April 1921. She had six other children, one that had passed away. She died tragically three years later, at age 30, while giving birth to her last child. Though Oscar had no living memory of his mother, he always regretted her death. His siblings told him it was his father's failure to provide needed medical care to his mother while she was giving birth to her last child that resulted in her untimely death. The agony of losing his mother so early in his development produced a profound heartache that persisted throughout Oscar's life.

Oscar's childhood was troubled and erratic. Even as a young boy, Oscar nursed a healthy hatred for his father, not only for his mother's early death but also for his father's failure to keep the family together after his mother's passing. Oscar could not and would not forgive his father's indifference to his young, motherless children.

His older sister Lilia tried to hold the family together, but there were six children—too many for her to manage alone—and Lilia herself was not yet grown. Oscar's father was not around to help. A railroad man, he was away for extended periods of time working as a mechanic along the various Southwest routes of Southern Pacific.

The first train had reached Tucson on March 20, 1880 as part of Southern Pacific's rush to expand throughout the Southwestern United States. This development opened up new work opportunities for those living in the area who had limited experience and education. Oscar's father, Jesus M. Lopez, was born in 1887 and was one of the early beneficiaries of Southern Pacific's expansion into Southern Arizona. They hired him early on as a mechanic, and for the times, it was a secure well-paying job.

After his wife died, Jesus seemed lost and untethered to his family. When home and not on the road, Jesus spent much of his time in the local bars drinking away his wages and worries, leaving the children to fend for themselves. Sent to track his father down at neighborhood pubs, Oscar would scour the area hoping to retrieve money for food before it was all dissipated in drink. The children had to live with various relatives after their mother's death. Many of the relatives were poor with children of their own to house and feed so the food money was a constant need.

The six kids were moved often from place to place depending on who could provide the best care for them. Never housed all together, the Lopez children were pretty much on their own at young ages. Each child experienced occasional tough times finding food and clothing. They often had no shoes to attend school. Because of their circumstances, the children did not get the attention and medical care they needed. They missed the loving devotion a mother and father could provide. This was difficult for all the children, and particularly hard on Oscar.

Jesus Lopez kept drinking even as the children grew older. A dedicated alcoholic, he had sporadic contact with his children. They were not fond of or attentive to their father, as they had been too intent on trying to sustain their own lives as they were growing up. One day, Jesus passed out on the railroad tracks and an oncoming train hit him. Critically injured, he was taken to the local hospital where he died a few days later. The then 24-year-old Oscar rushed to the hospital in time to see his dad before he passed away. Years later, Oscar recounted how he excoriated his dad on his deathbed for failing to take care of his children, for his excessive drinking, and for neglecting to provide the medical care his wife critically needed while giving birth to her last child. Oscar's father was 59 years old at the time of his death.

Oscar's early childhood, with its chaotic moving from family to family, only allowed him six years of formal schooling. Kicked out of school for being insolent to his teachers, Oscar was happy to leave school. That he had no suitable shoes to wear to school, embarrassed and angered him, adding to his frustration about his early schooling experience. Quick tempered from an early age, Oscar would stand up to anyone, adult or kid, who dared to challenge him. His pugnacity would come to haunt him through many later life events. He often came across as arrogant, which was more reflective of his trying to hide the intense sense of inferiority that shadowed him wherever he went. It was Oscar's way of bolstering his self-confidence. He felt he had to be in control of himself and his environment at all times.

CHAPTER 9

Oscar thought his teachers were idiots. Outright discrimination against Mexicans was rampant in Tucson in this era. The presumption was that all Mexican children had lice, so periodically the school wrapped thin cotton bands about two inches wide around the Mexican children's foreheads and then sprayed their heads with a toxic bug spray. The cloth headband was supposed to prevent the spray from running into their eyes; however, the cloth quickly became saturated and drips seeped down their cheeks and noses. Recounting those horrendous days, Oscar would say more than the physical harm caused by the dangerous spray was the shame the children felt as they were required to walk around the schoolyard with the damp, soiled cloth visible to the other school children.

This may be the reason that from an early age Oscar decided he was not Mexican. Oscar spent a lifetime telling anyone who would listen that his ancestors were the original Arizona settlers long before Mexico occupied the state and well before its official statehood occurred on February 14, 1912. He always spoke of being a fifth-generation Arizonian with an Irish and Native American background.

Oscar most likely did not know that his father was not born in Arizona but in San Miguel de Horcasitas, Mexico, as the official records show. Information on his mother was not available and perhaps there was a longer history on the maternal side. He claimed that his great

great-grandfather came from Ireland to Arizona. Shipboard records corroborated that his great great-grandparents left Ireland and settled in Arizona. So, Oscar did indeed have Irish blood. Subsequent DNA testing of Connie's children confirmed the Irish bloodline in the family.

From an early age, Oscar scrounged for work to survive. He was pretty much on his own as were all his brothers and sisters. He visited his sisters from time to time to share meals. Edna, the youngest, had fainting spells and was ill much of the time. She remained in chronic poor health throughout her adult life, most likely because she did not receive adequate preventative medical treatment as a child. Eventually, she was diagnosed with epileptic seizures as an adult.

None of the children received sufficient medical or social support as youngsters. Lilia, the eldest, tried to sustain her brothers and sisters in their younger years. She continued to be the heart of the family and the anchor that Oscar and his siblings needed. His three other brothers, Alfred, Rudy, and Manny had signed up to serve in the Armed Forces. Rudy left and became an Air Force pilot, choosing to make the service his life career, escaping far from home and his early years.

While in Tucson, Oscar rested, visited with family, and caught up with news about his brothers who were still overseas. He saw old friends, including a dear childhood friend, Julia. Years back when they were young children in school together, they had been close. They had made a pact agreeing they would marry upon reaching adulthood. Oscar went along with the promise, since he was fond of Julia. They knew each other's heartaches—both had suffered early in life. Julia believed that oath and would one day hold Oscar to it. But in January 1945, Oscar merely wanted to spend time with Julia as an old friend. He was not thinking of marriage, just renewing an old friendship. Marriage, in fact, was the last thing on his mind.

CHAPTER 10

While in Tucson, Oscar continued to worry about taking care of the marriage business. He never had enough money to do it while overseas, and he had not seen the point since it could wait until he returned to the States. One thing was exceedingly clear to him—he did not want to be married, just as he had told Connie when she initially asked. He definitely did not want to be married to someone who wanted no one to know about the marriage. Now he was back, he would see Connie and get it straightened out.

A little over two-and-a-half years had elapsed since he had last seen her. He had received no letters while overseas except the one letter asking him not to send letters addressing her as Mrs. Oscar Lopez. Connie did not know Oscar was back in the States and Oscar did not want to see her until after he spent a little rest time with his family. They did not know he was married, either. Not that Oscar was keeping it a secret; rather, it was that there was nothing to say about it except he had been a fool, and he would rather keep that to himself. Oscar was a proud man and hated to admit he had been tricked, even to himself. He wasn't sure why he wanted to wait to see Connie, but he went with his gut feeling on this. He might just give her a piece of his mind when he saw her, too.

After returning from his family visit, Oscar would go to Los Angeles to see Connie, file the paperwork there, and return to Tucson once discharged him from the service. He heard from his Uncle Joe, who still lived in the old neighborhood in L.A. that Connie and her sisters had never left even though her two brothers moved back to Mexico with her mother and father. Her younger brother, Tony, had stayed behind, as he was too young to serve. He enlisted in the service after the war.

Oscar could not fathom the whole point of the marriage since he now knew the sisters and Connie had remained in Los Angeles. As far as he was concerned, the marriage would be annulled. Uncle Joe told him that after Connie's mother left, the four Martinez sisters moved into an apartment together; but thereafter, Lucille left to get married and only Carmen, Ruthie, and Connie lived there now.

CHAPTER 11

Oscar returned to Camp Haan in mid-January 1945 to his job as a military policeman, where he spent his time corralling lonely soldiers back to the base. Embarrassed, they would tell him they were just looking for a little fun away from home. Oscar understood their reasons, but his orders were clear—keep the soldiers near the base and away from the brothels. The bordellos had their allure with liquor and lots of willing women. The soldiers knew the dangers, but boredom, lust, and restlessness egged them on.

Oscar knew he had to return to Los Angeles to see Connie and tell her of the annulment. He would have to do it on a weekend because his recent leave had used all his allowable release time. One Friday in late January 1945 after work, Oscar boarded the train to Los Angeles where he planned to stay at Uncle Joe's in his old bedroom.

On arrival, Oscar rummaged through the old dingy dresser drawers looking for the telephone number Connie had given him years before. He was certain he had tossed it in there when he was packing his duffle bag for overseas. He was not sure the slip of paper would still be there; however, Uncle Joe was not much for cleaning up or throwing things out, so it might still be there. Carelessly tossing his old clothes into a heap on the floor, Oscar found the yellowed piece of scrap paper in a bottom drawer. He would see if the number worked. If not, he would wander through the old neighborhood and see what he could find out. He did not have much time, only the weekend.

Oscar heard Connie's parents had sold the grocery store right before they left for Mexico with her two older brothers. Oscar wondered if her brothers would return once the war was over and if someone would hold them to some type of mandatory military service if they returned. *It doesn't seem fair*, he thought to himself. He had been drafted and done his duty. He later learned that Frank and Alfred never returned to the United States.

First things first! Oscar thought to himself. He needed an annulment, a divorce, or something. He would then move on with his life. Truth was, he was tired of being poor and he had high hopes of being somebody and having enough money to enjoy his life. After settling this marriage business and being released from the service, he would look for the best job he could get. Dialing the number on the scrap of paper, he took a deep breath, unsure of what would happen.

A woman with a high squeaky voice answered. "Hello, hello," she yelled into the phone several times. Guessing it might be one of her sisters, he firmly said, "Let me speak to Connie."

"Who is this?" the voice demanded.

"Let me speak to Connie," he growled, losing patience but recognizing it would be best not to identify himself as the missing husband.

"Hold on," the voice said. "I'll get her." He could hear a whispered conversation in the background with a squeaky voice saying, "He wouldn't give me his name."

Finally, after nearly two-and-a-half years they would speak.

"Hello," Connie said, in a tenuous voice.

"Hello, Connie, do you know who this is?" asked Oscar.

"No," she replied. "Who are you?"

Blood pounded in his head as Oscar realized she had responded honestly. Connie did not know who he was.

"It's Oscar, and we need to talk."

She seemed surprised although Oscar could not tell if Connie was pleased or not to hear from him. She gave him the address, and they agreed to meet the following afternoon. The next day, he rang the bell to the sisters' apartment. It worried Oscar that this would not be an easy conversation. He was still bitter about the whole occurrence.

Oscar arrived in full dress uniform, believing it gave him greater gravitas to do what he came to do. He rang the bell again. Ruthie, Connie's sister, answered. The whole family knew him from his grocery store days and she seemed surprised to see him, particularly when he asked for Connie. After greeting him, Ruthie asked him to have a seat saying she would tell Connie he was here. Running upstairs Ruthie returned a minute later announcing Connie would be down shortly.

Ruthie asked Oscar if he wanted something to drink. He was nervous, but he was not sure why, so he gladly agreed. She offered tequila. Oscar graciously accepted the drink, then a second and a third one. Whether from exhaustion, nervousness, or the liquor having gotten the better of him, Oscar could not divine. The reason did not matter; the unfortunate result was the same—Oscar fell asleep on the couch in Connie's apartment. He awoke to Carmen rushing down the stairs the next morning.

As a greeting, Carmen said, "Connie will be down soon."

"What happened?" he asked.

"I think you had too much to drink, and we didn't want to wake you. Bye," she said, as she slipped out the front door and left.

Likewise, Ruthie came downstairs, said she was leaving, and that Connie would be down soon. Oscar was not feeling well. His stomach was queasy. He had a crick in his neck from sleeping on the sofa, and he was a wrinkled mess. Hearing a noise, he turned to see Connie gliding down the stairs. It took all of Oscar's self-control not to berate his wife before she completed her descent, but before she reached the bottom stair, Oscar could no longer contain himself, shouting, "Why didn't you write me?"

"I figured you were angry when I asked you not to address the letters in my married name but didn't know what to say to you to get past that. It worried me. I prayed for your safety every night. You didn't believe me when I tried to explain why I didn't make it on our wedding night. I had planned on meeting you as we had agreed."

"Please, Connie, save it. You left me out in the cold when I was in the worst parts of the world without a single word…not one word. You were more concerned about getting in trouble with your mother for being married than contacting me or offering any kind of support. Yes, me, the person who did you a huge personal favor that you will recall I didn't want to do. This whole thing is unbelievable."

"Anyway, I am not sure why I am talking to you about this. It's all water under the bridge. I am getting an annulment. This marriage was a big mistake, and you didn't even leave the country. What the hell was that about?"

"Oscar, please, can you let me explain?" Connie said crestfallen.

"No, there is nothing to explain, it doesn't matter. I am finished with this business and will file the paperwork to annul the marriage. That's all I came to tell you. I am not feeling well and I have to go. I am already late reporting back to the base."

"Oscar, I thought we could have a nice life together. Is there anything I can say to you to change your mind or to convince you to give me a chance to make our marriage work?"

"I fell for your line once. Not again."

"Okay then. Can you at least wait here for a moment?"

Connie dashed upstairs. Oscar stared at her, unsure what the delay was about, but he waited, though not too patiently. Slowly walking down, the steps, she said, "I thought we could use this to start our life together, but since we will not do it, it's yours."

She handed him a small black savings book. The name on the passbook said, "Mrs. Connie Lopez."

He looked at it for a moment and then opened it. The amount in the account shocked him. It was more money than he had ever seen in his entire life—$900, which was more money than Oscar had ever envisioned or held in his hands.

"I saved every penny I received from the service pension for our life together. It's all there," she said sorrowfully, then turned away so he wouldn't see the tears in her eyes.

"How did you get the money," he asked, "if you weren't getting mail in your married name?"

"Oh," she said, "I got a post office box and picked up the checks there."

It occurred to Oscar that she could have also received his letters at the post office box, but he dismissed it since it did not matter now. Oscar would later recount to his eldest daughter his stunned reaction to the large amount Connie had saved and how tempted he was to take the money. He told Connie he had to sit down as he had a bad hangover from the previous night's drinks. As he sat there, he tried to think. He could not take the money from her. It was her money.

Looking up, he said, "Well, maybe we can try."

Pleased, Connie looked at him with a surprised smile. They would start a new life together. *Still, I don't know him, but I know I can love him. Would he learn to love me after all that already occurred?* she worried. Dismissing these thoughts, she reminded herself that all was possible with love, even happy endings.

Years later, Oscar would say it had been a terrible mistake to allow money to persuade him. His decision that rainy early January morning in Los Angeles affected so many lives.

CHAPTER 12

Connie's sisters guessed something was up by Oscar's sudden appearance and his strange behavior. Connie would have to advise her family of her married status, but she knew it would upset her mother. She could count on her dad's support, though he would not dare cross his wife, who ruled the household. Maria was a strong-willed woman. She had to be. Having nine children, two of which died in early childhood, made her that way. To make sense of her life in "el otro lado" (the United States), she believed she had to maintain strong control over her children.

Maria's children feared her, so they scrupulously followed her rules. Once adults on their own and out of the house, she still required them to call her every day and visit her once a week. It was an issue of respect and no exceptions were tolerated.

Maria had grown fond of Oscar as he came into her market often and was a friendly patron. To Maria, he appeared to be a lonely young man, both compelling and polite. All that would change once Connie's mother discovered the news about their clandestine marriage. Connie was intimidated by her mother but to start her new life, she would have to tell her. She would enlighten her sisters that afternoon when they returned home from work. They would defend her but not dare to oppose their mother.

Ruthie was the first one home from work. On entering the small cozy apartment, she threw her coat carelessly on the back of the kitchen chair. Rushing up to her, Connie said, "Ruthie, I need to talk to you. I need your support."

Surprised by the outburst, Ruthie sat down in the nearest chair, crossing her stocking feet on the coffee table.

"Do I need a drink for this?" she asked glancing at Connie's anxious face.

"No, no, it is good news."

"You're not pregnant?"

"No," Connie laughed. "I'm married and have been for almost two-and-a-half years."

Ruthie's jaw hung slightly agape.

Overcoming her shock, she asked, "Why the secrecy all this time, Connie? It's Oscar, isn't it?" probed Ruthie.

"Well, I wasn't sure how our mother would take it and then he left the country, so it didn't seem that I needed to tell her."

Connie would not tell Ruthie the part about the money. She did not need to know. In fact, Connie told no one the rest of the story. Not once throughout the years did she ever reveal her proposal to Oscar or what happened that January morning.

Carmen was the next one home. As the door opened, Ruthie rushed down the stairs. She did not want to miss this. Making herself comfortable on the sofa she plopped her feet up again on the coffee table. Ruthie was not sure what Carmen's response would be, but she wanted to hear it firsthand for herself.

Carmen entered the apartment carrying a large paper bag of groceries when Connie rushed up to her and said, "I need to talk to you, Carmen."

"What is it Connie?" Carmen asked impatiently as she unloaded the groceries on the kitchen counter and opened the refrigerator door.

"I'm married and am moving in with my husband," Connie told her.

Carmen's eyes widened as she screamed, "What are you talking about, Connie? How could you be married? What nonsense! You don't even have a boyfriend!" She slammed the refrigerator door closed and stood staring at Connie, open mouthed.

"You are right. I don't have a boyfriend," Connie replied. "I have had a husband for almost two-and-a-half years now and I am telling you about it now."

"Not Oscar, I hope," Carmen screeched. "He is poor, though very handsome, I'll admit."

"Well, yes. I married him," Connie said somewhat defensively.

Carmen raised an eyebrow and said, "So that is why you made such a fuss about mail coming to you as Mrs. Connie Lopez. You told us it was a mistake, but it wasn't a mistake, right?"

Looking somewhat sheepish, Connie now admitted it wasn't a mistake, but that she was afraid to tell anyone, especially her mother.

"Speaking of our mother," Carmen said, "When are you going to tell her?"

"Soon, but I need your backup as well as Ruthie's and Lucille's."

"I wouldn't count on Lucille if I were you," countered Carmen.

"Why not?" asked Connie.

"I am not sure she likes him, and you know she always sides with our mother now that she's married and not living at home," was Carmen's response.

"You know, Connie, I think Carmen's right. Better not count on Lucille," Ruthie piped up. "You've got us. Though I am not sure how much that will help."

CHAPTER 13

Connie knew telling her mother would be no easy task, but it had to be done. And, what was the harm? It was official. Maria would not be happy that they had not married in a church and that her youngest daughter had been keeping it a secret all this time. Her sisters hadn't pushed Connie asking why the marriage had been such a big secret, but her mother would ask.

Connie would have to have her story together. What was she going to tell her mother? What reason could she give for her secrecy? There was no plausible reason other than the truth she could offer, so she would have to avoid answering the question even if that caused her more trouble.

Connie tried to focus on her joy. Yes, she was happy, the happiest she had ever been. She liked Oscar. Maybe she could even learn to love him, though his feelings for her were nowhere near love. Connie was sorry the money influenced him, but it was for them. Could she get him to love her? She was sure she could, but she had a lot to learn. She did not even know how to cook! Since she was the youngest, she had never been required to cook or do household chores like her older sisters. Her knowledge about being a wife was even more limited, but she would learn. A hard worker, she would do what it took to make it work.

Connie did not know Oscar well. He was attractive, had a temper, and was smart. That's all she knew. It would be an adventure. They would need to sit down and talk about next steps and finding a place to live. Oscar would need a job when he was released from the Army in October. Connie could keep working. They were young. It would work out. *Things would work out*, she repeated to herself over and over. Despite assurances to herself that all was well, Connie had a nagging feeling it might not be so easy. Brushing away her doubts, she reminded herself there was no reason to worry. Her life was finally beginning.

Maria had returned to the States after settling her sons in Mexico. Connie called her and asked her if she would be home that evening. Maria extended an invitation for dinner. As the youngest, Connie had always been Maria's favorite. She was more lenient with Connie than she had been with her older daughters.

A gifted seamstress, Maria could create refined garments with little effort, from wedding dresses to finished men's suits. She excelled in making men's dress shirts. Maria never forced her youngest to sew, so Connie did not acquire her mother's expertise. Connie showed little interest in learning to make garments, even aprons, her mother's bread and butter. Lacking sewing and basic domestic skills would be an issue of contention later in Connie's life.

Uneasy, Connie arrived at her mother's at 5:30 PM, a little early. She had given herself a pep talk on the way there, but she was not sure how she would approach the subject of her marriage. Her mother appeared to be in good spirits, which gave her a momentary sense of relief. Then her sister Lucille arrived with her husband. Connie greeted her sister and her brother-in-law even though their appearance filled her with dread. She had believed she would be the only one at her mother's house for dinner.

Seeing her surprise, Maria casually mentioned, "They were planning on coming to eat, too, before you called." Connie did not know what to do. She didn't want to discuss her marriage in front of Lucille and her husband. It would be awkward enough without additional parties present. Connie was not sure what Lucille's response would be especially after her sisters' speculations that she was unlikely to defend her marriage to Oscar.

This meant Connie would have to wait to talk to her mother. Perhaps, she thought to herself, she could go in the kitchen and talk to her mother privately. There was a danger that a big scene might ensue, which would cause Lucille and her husband to rush into the kitchen to see what was going on. That was not a possibility Connie was willing to take. She could not tell Maria her news this evening. Disappointed, she headed home soon after dinner.

On Connie's arrival home, Ruthie ran down the stairs asking excitedly, "Well, what happened? How did she respond?"

Connie shook her head. "I didn't talk to her. Lucille and her husband showed up for dinner and I didn't want to gamble on it. I'll go in a few days, but it must be soon. Oscar wants us to look for a place this weekend."

"Where are you thinking of moving to?" queried Ruthie, curious to know how far her sister would move from them.

"Not sure we can afford too much. So, we are considering the new trailer park in East L.A."

"A trailer? Really Connie? Do you think you could live in one of those things? Aren't they small and crowded?"

"I can try. I'd rather save our money than pay more rent."

"Always saving, that's you all right, Connie," Ruthie sarcastically joked.

"Well, yes, that is me, but who is it that always has to borrow from me because she is out of money?"

"Oh, Connie, that was just twice," quipped Ruthie, knowing that was not true.

At work the next day, Connie kept going over what words she should use to convince her mother it would be okay. She worked at the same accounting firm as Lucille. In fact, Lucille had gotten her the job there. Connie knew there was nothing she could say that would appease her mother. Her mother had her own ideas about marriage and how it was supposed it to work and Connie's ideas were not close to acceptable. *It's okay*, she told herself. *It is my life and I must make my own choices. My mother will accept my choice once she sees how happy I am.*

Connie scheduled another dinner with her mother, but this time asked her if anyone else would be coming over. When her mother said, "No," Connie asked if she could bring Ruthie. Perhaps having her sister with her would bolster her courage. Secretly, she hoped Ruthie's brashness would stymie the slew of criticism that likely would ensue. The sisters arrived early. Connie was queasy. *It doesn't matter what my mother thinks or says*, she kept telling herself. *I've already married Oscar and we will have a life together.* Still, Connie did not want to be on bad terms with her mother. Her approval and backing was essential to Connie's well-being.

Maria was bringing the plates to the table when Connie announced, "I have something I want to tell you."

Puzzled, her mother looked at her but did not reply as she placed dishes in front of Connie and Ruthie. Connie noticed her mother had made her favorite dish, chili verde with beans and rice. Connie thought it would be best to let her mother sit down before going on any further, so she waited until Maria brought her own plate of food to the table before continuing. Once seated at the head of the table, her mother looked at her and waited. Intenseness and weariness reflected on her face as she stared at Connie.

Connie swallowed twice, then began, "It worried me we would leave the country…" Realizing immediately that that would not work, she said, "I wanted to marry him before he left for overseas." This caused her mother's eyebrows go up sharply. "Well, what I mean is…I was worried about him leaving, so I thought if I married him it would help him while he was away."

Connie glanced fleetingly at Ruthie who was shaking her head slightly. She was blowing this. She tried to regroup quickly.

"What are you talking about Connie and who did you marry?" demanded her mother.

"Um, well you know him, and you like him," muttered Connie.

"Who did you marry, Connie, and why didn't you tell us?"

"I married Oscar Lopez, right before he left for overseas."

There, she had gotten it out. Her mother's face reflected a kaleidoscope of emotions—from shock to disbelief, then settling on pure outrage.

"When was this and why did you keep it a secret?"

"I…I thought since he left so quickly, I would wait until he came back to tell everyone," Connie stuttered.

"Did you get married in a church?"

"No, we had a civil ceremony."

"Did your sisters know?"

Ruthie had her head down now, so Connie couldn't see her face. Some help she was.

"No one knew," she whispered.

Her mother stiffened her back ramrod straight.

"What were you thinking marrying a man you hardly knew? Did you tell your father?"

"I told no one."

Angrily, her mother asked, "Why are you telling me now?"

"I am telling you and everyone now because we are ready to start our life together."

"Is that your plan, Connie? You don't know the first thing about running a house or cooking," her mother said pointedly and though it hurt her, Connie did not respond.

What could she say? Without a doubt she had a lot to learn. Her mother seemed livid that Connie had pulled off a marriage without anyone knowing, but none of that mattered now. She had told everyone. She asked her mother to let her talk to her father, so she could tell him herself.

"Your dad is fond of Oscar and will be gravely disappointed how this occurred," warned her mother. Connie and Ruthie gathered the dishes from the table and took them to the kitchen. Ruthie looked at Connie's ashen face as she gently patted her hand but said nothing.

As the girls left their parents' house and got on the bus at the corner, Connie asked Ruthie how she thought it went.

"What do you think, Connie? Not well. Mom was indignant and angry. I would let the whole issue lie for two days if I were you, Connie."

Yes, that was what she would do. She still had to talk to Oscar about their plan and talk to her dad and Lucille. She was not that close to Lucille, so she didn't worry about that discussion. No, it was her mother and dad she was most worried about. Well, she had done it and though it was difficult, she felt relieved it was over. It was the hardest thing she had ever done since asking Oscar to marry her.

Over the next week, Connie spoke to her dad and Lucille about her marriage. Her dad responded in his usual sympathetic and calm way. He was such a counter to her mother. Nothing seemed to upset him, while almost everything seemed to excite her mother if not done her way or with her consent. Lucille appeared astonished but not too interested. She was much too focused on her recent marriage; which Connie had heard was not going all that well.

CHAPTER 14

Longing to start her new life and leave the old one behind, Connie met with Oscar to discuss where they could live. When in Los Angeles on leave, Oscar stayed with Uncle Joe. Uncle Joe's place was too small for the couple and Connie had heard from others Uncle Joe was a mean-spirited difficult man. *No, they needed their own place,* Connie thought.

Oscar had mentioned that he wanted to return to Tucson to live and work. Connie was against moving to Arizona where she would be away from her family, friends and everything she knew. She wanted to live in Los Angeles where she had a job and Oscar could find work more easily.

Oscar's post as an MP would end in the fall when he would be discharged. He had been trying to find work. His limited education made it hard. He knew he should go back to school. The government was offering all kinds of scholarships and pensions to returning soldiers under a new G.I. Bill. Oscar was not sure he could do it because he felt insecure about having not gotten far in school. This lack of self-confidence would plague him throughout his life. In fact, Oscar was a bright young man, although he never trusted his own native intelligence.

At work, Connie divulged her new married status to several friends. The girls wished her well. She did not disclose that the wedding had happened in the past but let them think it had taken place recently. One work friend asked the "new bride" how many children she wanted—a reasonable question but one that threw Connie. She had given little thought about how big a family she wanted. Connie had heard having children was difficult, so she was not sure how she felt about it. Worried, because she really had limited information on childbirth, Connie had not talked about it with Oscar, either. *There was plenty of time to think about children,* she thought.

A young woman at work gave her a lead on a place to live. Connie planned on checking it out as soon as she could. Leaving work early later that week, she went to visit the studio apartment which was near Uncle Joe's place, not in East L.A. It cost $55 a month, which would be tight for them. The average annual wage in 1945 was $2,400. While they were not rich, Connie and Oscar were like most other young couples of their time. With her modest wages and his money from the service, they could pull it off.

The studio was tiny, but it would only be for the two of them and she would make it homey. The bigger problem was the timing. The place was available in February, maybe March if she stalled a little, but Oscar's military discharge was not until the first week in October. Connie could rent the studio, but she would be there alone unless her husband came up on weekends. Before making a commitment, she had to talk to Oscar. She did not want to be living in the place alone for an extended period.

Reaching Oscar by telephone was difficult, too. Oscar was not allowed to leave the base every weekend. With only two phones on the base, busy signals were frequent. Connie had to leave a message and hope that it got through to Oscar. She had left two messages for Oscar so far and was waiting to hear from him. When she finally reached him, they discussed if she should take the place or not. Oscar's response was an adamant 'no,' saying they should wait to get a place closer to his release date. So, Connie let the place go.

The marriage remained unconsummated, but it would happen once they landed in their own place. Still anxious about it, Connie was looking forward to being married and living with her husband. Oscar, too, was eager to be settled and have a family. He still had his doubts, but it would be so nice to have someone cook for him, do his laundry, and have someone to talk to when he felt lonely. He hoped the marriage would work out; the money Connie saved would help them start out better than many other young couples. He was grateful for the assistance it would provide.

Consummating the marriage was Oscar's priority and he had an idea. He would find a location where they could meet for a long weekend. Connie could come to Riverside, but he doubted she would want to come. Besides, Riverside was far from ideal —the area was seedy, the motels and hotels unseemly. They were used for quick encounters by the local girls and servicemen. That is not what he wanted for his wedding night. No, it would have to wait. He wanted something better for their first time.

Oscar would also have to tell his family he was married, but there was no rush. Connie had not heard from her mother for a week, not since her big announcement.

No doubt her mother was still worked up about their marriage. Better to stay away from Maria a while longer. Surprised that her sisters were not more excited about her news triggered feelings of rejection on Connie's part. *Maybe it is because of our mother,* Connie rationalized. *Perhaps they know she would hold it against them.* Connie made all kinds of excuses for them, but it still hurt.

As February dragged into March, Oscar resolved to see Connie more. Telephone calls and whirlwind weekend dinners were not enough. Connie was his wife and he hoped to have a place where he could visit her and get to know her better and ultimately more intimately. During their next conversation, he asked her to start looking for housing so she could settle in and he could visit her on weekends when not scheduled to work. Connie learned of a trailer available in April but that would mean she had to pay the rent for seven months before Oscar could move in. It cost more than the earlier place—$65 a month. *Maybe he can help pay part of the rent,* she wondered. When asked, Oscar eagerly agreed to help, so Connie decided to take it.

Half-heartedly, Ruthie helped Connie haul her belongings to the dilapidated trailer. On first seeing Connie's new residence, she tried to hide her reaction by turning away from Connie. *No need to hurt her intentionally.* Ruthie did not like Connie living in a trailer and that one in particularly was unappealing, at least to Ruthie. Connie didn't notice her sister's revulsion. Luckily, Connie did not have much to move except her clothing.

She had no furniture or kitchen appliances. Lucille offered her a small kitchen table and Connie was sure she could pick up chairs at the local Goodwill Store around the corner from her mother's house. As she unpacked her stuff, Connie looked around the camper with a critical eye. Cramped and in desperate need of painting, it would be okay for two people. It would be theirs and the thought made her happy.

Oscar requested the first weekend in April off, so Connie was scrambling to make the mobile home welcoming for his upcoming arrival. He had not seen the vehicle but had heard details about their new home. It was located in a trailer park with a dozen other similar vehicles and sat in the northeast corner of the lot. A couple of bedraggled plants sat in terra cotta pots outside the front door. Inside, the actual studio space included no separation between the bedroom, kitchen, and living room. Oscar had mentioned that he thought $65 a month was high, but Connie reassured him it was the best she could find. Oscar could not complain since Connie had done the searching and made the final arrangements.

Connie absentmindedly cut the rubber band on the two bunches of miniature yellow and white daisies she had bought to brighten her home. Arranging them into an uneven bouquet, she placed them in an antique vase she found on her Goodwill trip. It had a slight chip on one corner, but if you turned that side to the wall it was hardly visible. Happy with her new creation, she sat it on the dresser nearest the bed and breathed a sigh of relief. Her new duvet with big, bold yellow flowers brightened up the place considerably. *Perhaps all this was too frilly for a man,* she thought to herself. *I hope he likes yellow.* She wanted to make it warm and welcoming for his arrival. She glanced around proudly one last time to see if there were any other changes she could make. It was the best she could do given her limited budget.

Oscar still had spent no real time alone with Connie, only telephone conversations and dinners since marrying. He wanted to move things along and now that Connie had gotten their new place secured, he would make it a point to get there as often as possible.

CHAPTER 15

Connie made a run to the grocery store to purchase food for their tiny white old fashioned icebox. At the store she remained puzzled and unsure what to purchase. She didn't know what foods Oscar liked or disliked and she felt shaky about the cooking part. She hadn't told him how little she knew about food preparation, though she had hinted that she might need help until she learned.

Connie opted for two small tomatoes, onions, hamburger, a cut-up chicken and milk and beer. She knew he liked beer because of his frequent purchases at the grocery store. Enthusiastic about Oscar's first visit to their new home, Connie trusted he'd like their dwelling. She tried so hard to fix it up and make to make it as cozy as possible.

What if he doesn't like it, she worried. *He has to love it. It is our new home and I want him to see it as I do. Yes, it's small, but it is ours and we are beginning our life together. Oh, dear God,* she prayed, *help him see it as I do.*

Oscar arrived the first week of April 1945. Dusk was approaching and the sun cast a golden glow as it descended. This gave the place a welcoming sepia appearance. He knocked and entered, plopping his dusty overstuffed duffle bag on the bed. Connie was in the kitchen stirring something on the stove. She looked appealing with her hair tied up and her full focus on the pot in front of her. She turned and gave Oscar a big smile. Grabbing her, he kissed her lightly at first and then more deeply. Perhaps it would all work out. Her dinner of chicken with tomatoes and onions was not bad. *I can do better, though,* he thought to himself. Oscar was an admirable cook, having learned at an early age. Wisely, he chose not to say much about the meal. There was plenty of time for her to master the kitchen arts. He would help her.

After their leisurely dinner, Connie knew there would be no more delays and that their marriage would be consummated that evening. That part of marriage—the physical intimacy between a husband and wife—had been something she was unsure of. Being unfamiliar with what she would have to do caused her to be off balance and her fears about sex surfaced, but Connie liked her husband and believed he would help her through her awkwardness.

For her special night, Connie had taken care to purchase a pale peach negligee, which she had placed discreetly on the back hook in the bathroom before Oscar's arrival. Gently laying her dinner dish in the sink, Connie excused herself and proceeded to the bathroom, closing the door behind her and locking it.

Standing in front of the medicine cabinet mirror, she scrutinized her pale face. *I can do this,* she told herself. *I might even enjoy it.* Her stomach fluttered uncontrollably. *Calm yourself,* she repeated as she pulled her new negligee over her slim shoulders. *I guess I have to take off my panties,* she thought as she slipped out of them. Once again, she gazed in the mirror and saw her eager and frightened face. Taking deep breaths, Connie unlocked the door and dashed towards the bed.

Surprised to see Oscar still sitting at the table sipping his beer, Connie stopped. Oscar seemed equally amazed to see Connie appear before him in her negligee. Noticing the worried look on his wife's face, Oscar's response was one of tenderness. Standing up, he reached for her, hugging her close to him. He could feel her trembling. He kissed her and told her not to worry. Slowly he led her to the bed, pulling the duvet covers down. He whispered to her to lie down and relax. He would be back shortly. Turning, he headed for the bathroom. Connie lay in the bed, not moving a muscle, waiting, barely breathing.

Then, unexpectedly, she heard the shower turn on. Laughing, she sat up in bed. *Here I am ready, worried to death, and he's taking a shower. Okay,* she told herself again, *calm down, everything will be okay.* After a quick rinse, Oscar wrapped a bulky white towel around his waist and headed to his waiting wife. He embraced her ardently, kissing her deeply. Connie was enveloped in Oscar's arms and soon relinquished her alarm and sighed contently. She did her part willingly and lovingly.

Oscar was not surprised that Connie was a virgin. Looking back at her wedding night, Connie thought she might have enjoyed it more had she known what to expect. Connie wished her sisters had at least filled her in on the personal details of married life. There was never a chance her mother would have told her anything, but her sisters could have gotten her better prepared. Overall, she felt contented that married part of her life had started.

The following month, Connie became pregnant with their first child. She did not know she was expecting and when she discovered it, she was not sure how she felt. She was excited, elated and terrified all at once and in varying degrees, depending on the time of day. Connie did not know much about children, but she could learn, just as she could gain cooking and household management skills. How difficult could it be? In retrospect, Connie realized she and Oscar should have discussed his feelings on how many children he wanted. There were many important life decisions they had not talked about.

A baby, she thought to herself, *how exciting!* She could not wait to tell the girls at work, but she had to tell Oscar first and then her family. The girls at work would talk and her sisters would hear about it. She could not risk them telling her mom before she did. Connie believed her mother would not be happy to learn of her pregnancy. Being mid-May, Connie figured the baby would be born in January of the new year.

She waited to tell her husband about the pregnancy. Part of her reluctance to share the news with Oscar had to do with her mixed feelings about the pregnancy. *I'm just not ready,* she thought to herself. *I just got married and am trying to figure a lot of stuff out. I am not sure how to be a mother,* the insecure part of herself repeated in her head. She tried to shush these thoughts as they flickered about. Sometimes she prayed hoping to chase away her fears.

Oscar tried to get home as often as he could on weekends, but he was often scheduled to work Saturdays and Sundays, so he could not always make it to Los Angeles. Connie found herself alone in the trailer trying to figure out how to tell Oscar about the pregnancy and wondering if he would be excited about her news. In between, she visited her mom and sisters to pass the time when not working. Always surrounded by a large family, Connie had rarely been alone for extended periods, much less lived alone. She was not used to being by herself. She was impatient for her new life to start and wanted Oscar around to share their new home.

Connie was a quiet, shy young woman despite her audacious proposal to a man she scarcely knew. She, like others in her generation, were 'Silent Knowers' who experienced the world through a veil of silence. Raised to believe they had no voice in important life matters many failed to gain their own authentic voice in their early years at home. As they grew to adulthood this reluctance to speak continued.

Connie remained passive throughout her marriage. Raised to believe that her voice had no value, she despised conflict and refused to argue with Oscar. Connie remained obedient to her mother, to the dictates of the church, to Oscar, to her doctors and to all authorities. Subdued, she repressed her grief and despair. She did not challenge others for fear they would not hear her. Connie also lacked confidence in her ability to learn new things, even relatively simple ones, and she would back away from new learning opportunities when presented.

Connie wanted to tell the world about the baby. It was hard keeping this important information in her heart. She hoped Oscar would be happy. Connie could not wait until they released Oscar from the service to tell him. Practicing the words she would use, Connie was not even able to explain to herself why she was so apprehensive. Mostly, she was fearful of his response because she had no inkling about how he felt about children. She resolved that the next time he came for the weekend and they went out for dinner, she would reveal her secret.

CHAPTER 16

The war ended on September 2, 1945 but Oscar's release would not be until October 10th. Oscar had six months left in the service. He knew he had to find a job prior to his formal discharge. During his next trip to Los Angeles, he intended on checking out a lead that one of his service buddies had given him. The position was for a molder at a local brass foundry. In the 1940s, large foundries were expanding their work in casting iron and steel as new markets were evolving. Iron and aluminum were being introduced into many new products for American households.

His friend had explained it was a tough job working in humid conditions requiring lots of physical exertion. But, hell, he was young and strong and he hoped they would hire him. He discovered at the interview it was not well-paying, but it was a job. Oscar told them he could not start working until his release. More than likely, the foundry would still have openings in late September/October since it was not an easy or desirable job. Oscar was pleased when he received a call back advising they could hire him as a molder starting in mid-October.

The foundry produced metal castings and the heavy labor required many workers. They ran the furnaces, heated the individual cut up metal pieces into liquids and poured the liquid metal into molds. The intense heat from the furnaces, along with massive quantities of molten metal being moved around in large containers made for very dangerous working conditions. Not only did heavy black smoke from the melting iron fill the air, but workers could see flames shooting out of the edge of the furnaces because of the high temperatures required. Few safety checks were in place and accidents happened, often serious ones, but as Oscar observed, no compensation was available for injured workers as state and federal laws to protect workers had not yet been enacted. Injured workers were on their own.

Oscar returned home from work exhausted, his face blackened from the smoke. He and the others appreciated their jobs and worked hard. In Oscar's case, it paid the rent on the trailer. Oscar valued the physical effort required each day because he liked hard work, but he craved a more lucrative occupation, one that did not leave him so exhausted that all he wanted to do was sleep. Nevertheless, he worked at the foundry until he left California.

Manny, Oscar's brother, called and left him a message saying he wanted to talk to Oscar about a possible job. Oscar was eager to hear what his brother had to say about other professions. Excitedly, Manny relayed information about the position as a floor installer, the same work Manny did. The hourly wage was higher and there were benefits. Oscar had no health benefits in the factory. The problem was that the position was where Manny lived in Tucson. This meant leaving Los Angeles.

Making more money appealed to Oscar as he spent as much money as he made, and sometimes more than he made. Money became a point of contention between Oscar and Connie early in the marriage. Connie was careful with her money, watching every penny. If Oscar needed a truck, he wanted to get a new one even if he did not have the money to do it. Oscar felt he worked hard, and was entitled to have something reliable to get around in. He did not believe in depriving himself. Just thinking he might pull off getting a new truck got Oscar excited about the job outlook. Maybe he would take up Manny's offer to get him hired as an apprentice in the local shop in Tucson. The only problem was he would have to tell Connie they needed to move. He knew she wanted to stay in Los Angeles.

CHAPTER 17

The girls in the office held a baby shower for Connie before she left work, which pleased Connie immensely. At the shower, one of her friends asked how many children she wanted. For a moment, Connie hesitated, realizing she did not know. Also, she was aware of how it would sound if she said one child might be enough. The office girls noticed Connie did not respond, but they excused her failure to reply as being overwhelmed with the prospect of becoming a new mother.

Birthing procedures in the 1940s required women to recuperate for one full week in the hospital and longer for cesarean procedures. New mothers were supposed to be completely rested before returning home. Connie was completely anesthetized for the delivery. Upon awakening, a red-faced swaddled baby was thrust into her arms. Connie felt an immediate outpouring of love for her helpless infant. The newborn nudged her head toward Connie's left breast. Afterwards, the baby was kept separately in the nursery and brought to Connie only for feeding for short periods of time. Bottle-feeding was considered the best option at this time.

When his daughter was born, Oscar was ecstatic, but Connie had trouble adjusting to her new life with the new baby. She wanted to be the best mom she could be, but managing the house, cooking, and taking care of the baby was harder than she had dreamed. It did not help that she did not know much about the care of babies. After a few months, Connie was sure that one child was about all she could handle. She had to admit to herself that she was not crazy about babies, but she kept her feelings to herself. She knew everyone loved babies. Connie worried about getting pregnant again but had no one she could confide in about her concerns.

Connie thought of marriage in romantic terms. With no knowledge of the day-to-day workings of relationships or managing a household, Connie was learning quickly that the reality was different. Her cooking was improving, but was nowhere near Oscar's expectations. She was not faring much better in maintaining their small trailer. It seemed there was always something to do and try as she might, she could not get everything done. She was often brought to tears with her effort. Connie daydreamed it should be easier. She chided herself for her slowness in managing household matters. *Why*, she asked herself, *can't I do the dishes swiftly and get them done? None of this is so hard,* she reminded herself, *just do it and stop thinking about it.*

Despite this, things were going well with she and Oscar. They finally had that much-needed conversation about children. Astonished and alarmed, Connie learned that her husband wanted as many children as possible.

As the baby grew older, things improved. Still unhappy about the marriage, her mother asked Connie to bring the baby to see her from time-to-time, but without Oscar. After Connie revealed her secret marriage to Maria, her mother decided she hated Oscar. She never accepted the marriage, though she had never heard the entire story.

Maria never forgave Oscar, nor did she ever speak to him again.

When Connie visited, Maria had gifts for the baby. She had made a beautiful pale-yellow knitted garment and pastel-colored receiving blankets for her. Connie loved receiving goodies for the baby, but wished her mother recognized her marriage and could be more encouraging. It would make things easier. It continued to be important to her, though she never examined why on a conscious level or even understood how core it was to her happiness. Her mother's approval would continue to be something she yearned for entire her life.

With things as they were, Connie did not feel she could call upon her mother with questions about the baby and this made her life challenging. She had lots of things she wanted to know about crying babies, colic, and other trivial things concerning feedings and diapering. None of her sisters had children yet, so they could not help. She had one friend who had a little boy and she wanted to get together with her for coffee to get her questions answered. Yet Connie kept hesitating to extend the invitation. The truth was that Connie was shy when it came to be discussing personal matters, even though she needed all the advice she could get. She remained unaware of her inability to reach out to others for help and dismissed it as her failure to get organized.

When her daughter turned nine months old, to her horror Connie discovered she was pregnant. She became distraught. She was learning to hold it together with one baby, but she could not see how she could manage another child so soon. There were still lingering doubts of whether she wanted another child while trying to manage the other issues in her life. She had no one to talk to about her feelings. Her mother would get angry and be of no help. Her sisters could not relate to her having the first child, so who knew what they would say when they discovered she was pregnant again? Most likely, they would not offer words of comfort.

Connie went into the bathroom and locked the door. Sitting on the side of the bathtub, she tried to figure out why she was so fearful of another pregnancy. The earlier birth had not been painful. She was sedated for the entire birth and only awakened after the delivery when her baby was handed to her. She did not have to breast feed the baby. Connie had given her first daughter a bottle and would elect to bottle-feed all her later children.

Thinking it over, Connie decided she needed more time before having another child to rest and to figure things out. *Damn,* she thought, *I am still trying to make my way through the things I need to learn. I need more time!* she screamed in her head. *Everything would be better if I had more time to get used to my new roles.*

Scheduling an appointment with her doctor to confirm the pregnancy, Connie thought perhaps she was not pregnant, just late. *One could be hopeful,* she reasoned. *There are other reasons for your period being late.* Her goal was to discuss in detail with the doctor what could be done to avoid future pregnancies. She had not told Oscar yet about the pregnancy nor about her planned discussion with the doctor.

On the day of her appointment, Connie reviewed how she would discuss such an intimate matter with a male doctor. Asking questions of authority figures intimidated her. Yes, she was married, but she would have to admit to him she did not want more children, at least not now, and that would be tough. Connie was not even sure she had the words she needed to explain her predicament. The thought of it brought tears to her eyes. It frightened and worried her. She felt uncertain whether she could go through another pregnancy so soon. She prayed and prayed for an answer.

As Connie entered the doctor's office, the receptionist greeted her by name and asked her to take a seat. The waiting area was filled with many patients. Some were pregnant. Her doctor was older and often distracted as he performed his exams, at least on her, but she assumed he was that way with all his patients. She was hoping for more attention this time. After hearing her name announced, she followed the nurse to the inner examining room. She had just sat down on the exam table when the doctor entered. Connie explained she thought she was pregnant and needed confirmation. Then she added, "Doctor, I cannot have another baby so soon. My daughter is nine months old and will only be fourteen months old when the new baby is born. It is too much for me to handle."

Connie lay still on the examining table, trembling. She looked down, embarrassed, afraid to say anything more. The doctor stopped moving around the room and turned to consider her.

"Let's confirm you are pregnant first," he said. Looking skyward, Connie repeated a quick prayer to her favorite saint as he started his examination. She studied his face, trying to guess the answer, but it was inscrutable. He gazed up at her and said, "Yep, you are pregnant. You are two months along."

Startled by the confirmation, Connie looked into the doctor's eyes to see if she could discern a trace of kindness or concern for her situation, but he had already turned his back to her busying himself with her paperwork. Coughing to get his attention back to her, Connie asked again, "Doctor, is there anything I can do? There must be something."

"I'm not sure what you're asking, Mrs. Lopez," he said in a gruff and dismissive voice. Silenced by his tone, Connie looked down and said, "Doctor, this is very difficult for me. I am not sure I can have another child so soon."

"You don't have a choice," he said as he turned and left the exam room.

Angry and upset by his quick dismissal, Connie left the doctor's office. On the way home on the bus, she studied the other passengers' faces and wondered about their lives. Were they like hers? Were theirs easier? Harder? She did not understand what she would do. *It's okay*, she said to calm herself. *It's okay, it will be okay . . . it will be okay.*

The next day when Oscar came home, he found his wife crying as she sat rocking the baby in a chair near the door. Alarmed, he asked, "What's the matter? Is the baby okay?"

"She's fine, Oscar, but I am not. I'm pregnant!"

"Connie, that's wonderful news. Why are you so upset?"

"I am upset because it's too soon to have another baby. Our daughter's just nine months old and I am not sure I can handle two small babies at one time."

"Sure, you can," Oscar said "I'll help you. Babies are wonderful. It'll be okay." Oscar beamed, looking rather pleased with himself. Connie kept rocking the baby as tears continued to slide down her cheeks. Oscar stood near his wife observing her tears, unsure what he could do to calm her concerns.

CHAPTER 18

Connie stood in front of the stove making dinner, hitching the squirming baby on her right hip. The gurgling baby was trying to slide down and away from her mother towards the floor. Observing the scene pleased Oscar at a profound level. He had always longed for a family and the closeness it entailed. It was something he never had since losing his mother at an early age.

He was running out of time to talk to Connie about the job Manny was offering in Tucson. Instinctively, Oscar knew Connie would not be happy, but things were not good with her mother. And, the way he saw it, the change might be good for her, too. Oscar was glad to have a new job prospect and he yearned to return home.

He debated in his head the perfect way to bring up the subject, but couldn't come up with anything, so he figured he would say it straight out and see what happened. Oscar peeked over at Connie again and went to grab the baby from her. His daughter brought him so much joy. He bounced her up and down and she giggled. Connie turned around to look at her husband. Patting the table, he motioned for Connie to come sit in a chair.

"Connie, let's talk about a job prospect I have." Hesitating for a moment, he said, "Manny can get me a decent job that is more suitable than the one I have and it pays better. I think it would be great for us now with the baby and another one on the way. The job is in Tucson, so we would have to move. What do you think?"

Stunned, Connie's panicked thoughts came tumbling forth from her lips. "But my family is here. I know no one in Arizona!"

"My sisters and brothers are there," countered Oscar. "You'll love my two sisters, Lilia and Edna. They will help you."

Connie looked at him doubtfully. She did not want to move, even though she hadn't worked out her differences with her mother. She was pregnant with a baby due in May and was struggling with how she felt about another baby so soon. She could not tell Oscar that last part. He looked at her, patiently waiting for her response.

"Oscar, I don't think I can do it! I'm too weighed down with the baby, another pregnancy and now you want to move to another state?" she cried.

With that, Connie bolted from the kitchen table dashing headlong for the bathroom, slamming the door. She sat on the toilet seat crying. She had not locked the door and Oscar came in with the baby in his arms. He looked at Connie's tear-stained face and wondered what he could say to convince her it would not be so bad. They would have better housing in Tucson and his sisters could help with the kids. *The new pregnancy is throwing her off keel,* he thought to himself.

Just then, the baby let out a tremendous squeal. Oscar handed Connie the baby and tiptoed out of the bathroom. Connie squeezed the baby tightly, which made the child howl more. She rocked and shushed the baby as she headed back to the kitchen to finish making dinner.

Oscar dropped the subject for now. Today was not the day to push for the move, but he had to get back to Manny. He guessed he needed to act by the end of the year. Connie would only be four months pregnant then, he reasoned, not so far along to make relocating to another state unreasonably difficult. He believed they could do it. The next day at work, Oscar again pondered if moving was the best thing for him and his family. He wanted to go home. Connie would adjust. It will be a good change for her away from her family who had not given her that much encouragement and who had made it clear how they felt about him.

As she was getting dressed to go to church, Connie mentioned to Oscar that she would be going to see her mother afterwards. Oscar thought it best not to say anything because he knew Maria's anger toward him had not lessened. He'd prefer Maria knew less about their lives, rather than more, but it was up to Connie. He would stay out of it.

Connie worried about her relationship with her mother. Connie was settling into the idea of a second child now that the shock of the pregnancy had worn off. She had to tell her mother and her sisters that there would be another baby. Sheepishly, she had to admit she was excited that her daughter would have a playmate, but it scared her. How would she manage a second baby? Connie called her mom and arranged to see her on Sunday. Trying to be optimistic that her mother would be overjoyed with a second grandchild, Connie took the bus right after church.

She was hoping for a happier reception than had happened with the last birth announcement.

As Connie walked up the stairs to her mother's house, her dad greeted her at the door.

"How are you, my sweet *hija?*"

Connie hugged her dad, grateful for his unwavering support. Seeing her mother in the kitchen stirring pots, she rushed in to greet her with a smile, asking how she was. She debated if she should wait for her dad to come into the kitchen so she could tell them the news together, but went ahead and told her mother.

"I have good news I want to share with you and mi Papa," Connie blurted. "I am expecting another child. We are so excited!"

Her mom looked surprised. Then her face took on the stern, pinched expression so familiar to Connie.

"But why, Consuelo, you have a small child already? Isn't it too soon?"

"I know, but these things happen. Yes, I would have liked a little more time before having another child, but I am pregnant now. I was hoping you would be pleased for me."

"Consuelo, you know how I feel about Oscar. That will not change. I am concerned for you."

"Don't be. I will be okay. We are happy and I have other news," she mumbled. *Get the rest out,* she told herself firmly. Swiftly, she added, "We are moving."

Maria suddenly became more alert at this additional bit of news. "When are you moving?"

Connie's eyes watered as she said, "We are moving in about four months to Tucson. I will miss you and Papa."

When her father came to the table to eat, she relayed her news. He seemed surprised but did not say much except to congratulate her on her new little one. Her father's well wishes warmed Connie's heart and for the time being she felt more lighthearted about the situation. It would work out somehow. She believed that in her heart of hearts.

CHAPTER 19

On the bus ride home, Connie concluded she would tell Oscar she was ready to move. Though apprehensive about a relocation, she wanted to be with her husband and be a supportive wife. On her arrival home, Connie saw Oscar sitting in his favorite chair listening to the ballgame on the radio. Rushing up to him, Connie hugged him as she told him she was ready to move. Looking into her husband's eyes, Connie murmured she would need his assistance, though, for this to work.

The young Lopez family moved in December 1946 to Tucson amid a stream of goodbyes and well wishes. Connie's first daughter was almost a year old and thriving. Connie had high hopes for their new city, but was filled with disappointment with at the sight of their home in Tucson. Shielding her eyes from the blazing sun, Connie looked up to see a weather-beaten, dusty brown old camper that looked not much bigger than their trailer in Los Angeles. On entering it, she noted it only had minimal furnishings. She would do her best to fix it up, but the space was limited and with a new baby, it would be tight. Oscar was jubilant to be in Tucson. He saw it as a new beginning, telling his wife that the old trailer was only a temporary stop, and that once he got his new job they would find a bigger, better place.

Connie tried to keep her ambivalence to herself, but the trailer, with its numerous cockroaches, alarmed her. The new baby would be here soon, and Connie needed greater comfort in her home. She had not planned on working as she was well along in her pregnancy. As promised, Oscar had her meet his sisters soon after their arrival. Upon meeting Lilia, Connie felt a strong bond that would be the beginning of a great friendship, one that would prove to last for many years and through the trials Connie would face. She also met Edna, who was warm and welcoming but did not touch her in the same way Lilia did.

In May 1947, their second daughter, Christina, was born. Both Connie and Oscar were elated. Their firstborn, however, did not seem as pleased to have a rival for her parents' attention. She cast a dubious look at the newborn as she lay on the bed. Soon after settling in, Oscar got the job installing floors, which he enjoyed right away. It had no smoke or heat and the new job tested his mathematical ability. Oscar felt fulfilled by seeing the floors he worked on professionally finished. A quick learner, he took on more difficult assignments and ultimately became a master installer able to supervise and direct others.

Oscar took considerable pride in his work, later encouraging four of his six sons to follow him into the trade. Two sons did follow Oscar's footsteps becoming master installers themselves. The same two of them would start their own company. Years later, Connie's first and second sons, Mike and Daniel, told stories of working with their dad during the summer months when they were 13 and 14 years old.

Oscar gave the boys a quick demonstration on how to lay tiles and then watched them do several to ensure they mastered the process. He then sent his two sons off alone to the nearby newly-built, unoccupied houses to work on the entry and dining room areas. Meanwhile, he worked in one house doing the more difficult process of laying down linoleum called coving. He would cut a solid piece of linoleum to fit it in a small area, flush out the corners, then apply heat to get the corners straight. Oscar felt that the work was too complicated for his sons and he did not want them using the blowtorch.

With the help of both sons, the company soon became suspicious yet pleased with the large number of houses Oscar finished. When asked how he completed so many houses so swiftly, Oscar said he worked faster than other workers. This response did not satisfy management because the number of completed houses was far greater than any of the other installers. The company owners wanted to figure out what Oscar was doing differently than other installers so they could encourage the others to be as productive. Advising Oscar of their plans, the company sent staff out to Oscar's assigned locations without notifying him when they would be on site. Their job was to check on how he was saving time and report back to management.

Oscar alerted his sons to keep an eye out for the company truck. The housing projects were large and formal streets had not yet been installed, so the young men could hear the trucks rumbling along the make-shift dirt road as they headed toward the houses. This was the signal for the two boys to stop working and run and hide.

Company inspectors arrived at the first house, jumped out of the company truck and dashed into the house looking for Oscar. All they saw as they entered house after house were rows and rows of tiles neatly piled up and some partially laid areas but no one in sight. They would move on to the next house and again see tiles piled high in the dining room but no Oscar. Eventually, they would find Oscar in a house working in one the bathrooms. When asked why the houses were partially started and left unfinished, Oscar explained he was waiting for them to dry and in order not to waste time, he would move on to the next house, returning later to finish the job.

Somehow, they believed his story and the company never caught on to Oscar's game. His sons were not paid any money for their arduous work those summers, but Oscar allowed them to purchase all the food they wanted from the local lunchtime food trucks. Both sons agreed that full access to the food trucks was sufficient pay for them.

The company secured a contract to build military housing, which provided Oscar with even greater work opportunities. As a master installer, Oscar would become so well respected by his company, Tri-Way, he would be sent to various sites, including out-of-state locations, to supervise and run crews on special jobs. Highly regarded because he was hardworking and someone who could always be counted on to get the job done, he got many plum assignments. Oscar always needed more money with his growing family and his easy spending, so he worked as much overtime as he could.

Pride in work well done was important to Oscar who felt very insecure about his limited education. He spent a good deal of time reading, trying to educate himself. Oscar became active in the union and at one time was encouraged by management to pursue an open union steward position. He wanted to run. He knew the guys and he had their support. But Oscar was afraid that not having a high school diploma would hurt his campaign and would prove an embarrassment, so he declined. Oscar often reminisced about that lost opportunity. He knew it would have given him the recognition he craved.

Connie was adapting to her new life in Tucson, although she missed Los Angeles and her family. She was not sure how she felt about the hot weather, but she was getting support from Oscar's sisters and this meant a lot. She did not feel so alone. Oscar was content with his new job, being close to his family and occasionally working with Manny. He made it a point to buy a white pickup truck for work soon after his arrival home. It was his pride and joy and his first new vehicle. Connie continued to worry about money, knowing how difficult it was for Oscar to restrain his spending. She was learning to be thriftier and to manage every cent, something that would serve her well in future years.

Oscar loved baseball and was a serious fan. Sometimes he and the guys would play a game or two in a nearby field. At other times, he would sit in his truck listening to his favorite baseball team, the Dodgers. He never missed an opportunity to follow his beloved team even if it meant neglecting needed chores around the house. Peering out the kitchen window, Connie observed Oscar sitting in his truck with his ears plugged into the game. That day, October 6, 1947, the Yankees won over the Dodgers with a 4–3 victory. Oscar stomped into the kitchen passing Connie, unhappy with the game results. Connie had other things on her mind besides baseball and she wished Oscar did, too. Sighing, she returned to washing the dishes.

Connie was hoping they could take a trip to Los Angeles to see her family, but with caring for her two daughters and managing the household there did not seem to be enough time or money to make the outing. Connie even considered going alone to Los Angeles, but knew she could never leave the two girls with Oscar and she did not want to go without her husband.

Connie saw Lilia and her children often and they compared notes on household matters and shared meals. Lilia was an excellent cook known for her homemade flour tortillas and other specialty dishes. The children loved visiting so they could run and play with their cousins, but they especially loved Lilia's home-cooked meals. Food was always extra spicy, and the kids would sit at the table eating with tears running down their cheeks, grabbing hot tortillas to quell their heated mouths. Connie was feeling more relaxed about her role as a mother and was continuing to pick up cooking tips from Lilia, although she had to admit that she was still not fond of cooking.

Lilia and Connie became close devoted friends. Connie was disinclined to share too much personal information about her and Oscar's relationship for fear Lilia might mention it to him. The critical question Connie most wanted to introduce into her and Lilia's casual ongoing conversations was what she could do about contraception. Did Lilia have any knowledge that might assist her? But Connie did not have the daring or the wherewithal to do it, so she never risked voicing her inquiries out loud to Lilia. They remained unasked.

The friendship remained intimate, however, and served as a quiet place where Connie could be herself and share some of her other worries, if not all. Lilia generously imparted her vast knowledge about cooking, childcare, and household matters she had picked up at a young age. All this helped to reassure Connie in her role as a homemaker and mother.

CHAPTER 20

In May 1948, Connie discovered she was pregnant with her third baby. She had mixed feelings. This time she informed Oscar as soon as she discovered she was with child. For his part, Oscar was thrilled with the news. Again, Connie kept her fears and concerns to herself. They would need to move again because their place was too small for a third child. *It will be okay*, she told herself.

Connie naively believed she was happy with her life as long as it did not involve money discussions. Connie and Oscar argued constantly about money. A much bigger spender than Connie, Oscar would rather make a purchase on credit than save money to buy it, which was more consistent with Connie's way of thinking. Oscar would tell her he did not want to deprive himself. He worked hard and wanted to have the rewards of that demanding effort. Sometimes he did not tell her about purchases and Connie would find out when the bill arrived.

Connie's third child, Michael, was born in November 1948. A healthy baby boy, he came into the world with a full head of hair, looking around curiously at his new world. Early on he would develop breathing and asthma problems. The asthma attacks became more pronounced when the family later moved to Los Angeles from Tucson.

Enthused about the birth of his first son, Oscar insisted on naming his newborn Oscar, Junior. Connie refused, saying she did not want the child named after his father. Connie believed children should have their own individual names and stubbornly held her ground even though her rebuff angered Oscar. Many years later, Oscar's fourth son would carry his name.

By the time Connie and her children moved back to California, the air quality in Los Angeles had dangerously deteriorated. Smog alerts were issued regularly advising those with health issues to remain inside or in sealed-off areas to prevent breathing contaminated air. Many Angelenos had continued burning their trash in backyard makeshift incinerators rather than having it picked up. Even after stringent measures were put into place, it would take many years before the Los Angeles basin air quality significantly improved, although almost sixty years later smog continues to blanket the Los Angeles basin.

The smog often appeared as pale-yellow glow on the edges of the horizon. In early daylight, it gave the city an eerie look—buildings appeared as distant shadowy silhouettes even though they were a merely a hundred feet away. At night, it lingered low causing the city lights to reflect off of buildings of all sizes in disturbing ways. The smog brought tears to Connie's eyes and those of her children, affecting those with asthma.

Connie spent many a night holding her oldest son in her arms as he experienced acute asthma attacks, trying to soothe him and reassure him he would catch his breath and praying silently to the heavens to help her son breathe normally.

Though he used inhalers, Connie frequently had to rush him to the hospital for oxygen, taking three buses to reach the hospital since she did not have a car. Michael spent the whole time wheezing as they transferred from bus to bus. As he grew older, the attacks became less frequent, but they continued throughout his lifetime.

Soon, the Lopez family was preparing to move to larger housing. Connie's time was filled with packing and moving details. She now had three children under the age of five; it would be an understatement to say she had her hands full. Managing the house and children still presented problems for her, but she was mastering new cooking skills and adding recipes to her repertoire. Her kids fancied the applesauce muffins she made for them as a special treat, always begging her to make them more.

Connie loved her children but did not take time to embrace, hug, or reassure them of her love through any type of physical touch. It did not occur to Connie to do these things. Her own family had never shown her tangible affection or spoken to her in terms of endearment, so this was not something native to Connie's understanding of raising children. The children assumed their mother loved them, but Connie gave no outward demonstrative indications of her love.

Connie wondered about this sometimes as she silently observed other mothers cuddling and hugging their children in parks and other public places they visited. Still, she did not change her interactions with her own children. *Am I raising them correctly?* she thought. She found solace in thinking it must be right. *This was the way my mother raised us and we all turned out all right.*

The family moved to a slightly bigger place, but chaos still reigned. Oscar spent more and more time working, but he had another housing idea for his growing family. A new planned community was being developed on the outskirts of Tucson called Pueblo Gardens. The development contained a park and modern three and four-bedroom contemporary houses with large backyards. After discussing it and paying a visit to the partially constructed homes, Oscar and Connie decided that it would be a great place to raise the kids.

A brand new three-bedroom house awaited them in Pueblo Gardens. All they had to do was save the money for the down payment. In the meantime, they had to stay put in their cramped two-bedroom house. The thought of a larger home with additional space and a backyard for the kids was something Connie had only imagined. Thus far, they had only lived in crowded conditions. With so many little ones running around, this did not favor an orderly household.

Oscar made it clear he liked a tidy house, but just keeping the kids bathed and fed took most of Connie's time. Maintaining the house in pristine order was not on the top of Connie's list and it would never be one of her priorities. She liked the idea but did not have the energy to do it, and it was not as important to her as it was to Oscar.

Oscar and Connie's ideas about child rearing differed radically too. Oscar was a strict disciplinarian who expected his children to respond immediately to any direction given. He was quick to anger if they neglected to respond instantaneously and would threaten to spank them, although this was something he rarely did. Oscar's forceful voice heeded his children to mind him and obey his commands. If not, he would take off his belt with a great flourish while looking at the children. This would send them all scattering in all directions to avoid being hit. Connie was less authoritative. She would tell the kids to stop fighting and to stay out of trouble. If they continued to cause a ruckus, whining or fighting, she sent them all outside to play, then locked the door behind them.

A point of contention between Connie and Oscar early on was whether the children should learn to speak Spanish. Connie spoke Spanish and believed it would be good for the children to learn. Oscar did not agree. His Spanish was broken, which was only partly the reason for his reluctance. His real objection was due to his perception of who he was and who he wanted his children to be. Since returning from WWII, Oscar had embraced the John Wayne concept of what it meant to be an American. He wanted his kids to speak English only, to be "real" Americans. Speaking Spanish would not fit into that viewpoint, so he decreed no Spanish could be spoken in his house. That became the rule. Connie did not agree, but she did not argue. Her mother never let her forget that she had failed to teach her children Spanish.

Connie continued to speak to her eldest daughter in Spanish whenever she did not want the younger children to understand what she was saying. Her eldest daughter had a good understanding of the language, but was not fluent. The rest of the children had limited exposure. Acquaintances and friends often asked them why they didn't speak their native language. This question hurt the eldest daughter. She was ashamed that the family did not speak Spanish because she believed that when you lost your language, you lost your culture. She committed to do something about it when she grew up.

Yolanda knew it was way too late for her and brothers and sisters to learn Spanish or for some to even understand the importance of what they had lost. Perhaps the dream of recapturing their heritage would be possible for the next Lopez generation. Her children, she decided, would be the ones to return the Spanish language to the family.

Years later, she would make an agreement with her young twelve-year-old daughter that her future children would speak fluent Spanish. To insure this happened, she sent the young girl to Cuernavaca, Mexico and San Jose, Costa Rica for full Spanish immersion and then on to a Spanish-speaking country while she completed her junior year of college. Her daughter kept her commitment and not only became a fluent speaker but ensured her son would attend a Spanish bilingual school until age twelve.

CHAPTER 21

In May 1949, Connie suspected she might be pregnant again. The prospect of having another child distressed her. She already had three children: a seven-month-old boy, a two-year-old girl, and a three-year-old girl. Connie scheduled an appointment with a new doctor without telling Oscar. As she sat in the waiting room, she tried to decide what she could say to stop the pregnancies.

Hearing her name called startled her out of her reverie and reluctantly she followed the nurse into the exam room. Left alone, she felt tears start to spill down her face. She brushed them away with her hand and took a deep breath. *Please*, she prayed. *Help me. I cannot have another child so soon. I am not ready and do not think I can do it. Please*, she whispered gently into the air.

The doctor entered. He was younger and better looking than her former doctor. This gave her confidence that perhaps he would be more sympathetic to her plight. She informed him she needed to confirm if she was pregnant. Laying on the exam table, Connie wondered what his response would be. She knew she was pregnant, but she was longing for it not to be true.

On completing the exam, the doctor said, "You are just about four-and-a-half weeks along in your pregnancy."

Connie's eyes filled with tears as she asked, "Is there anything that can be done to end this pregnancy?"

Suddenly, the doctor glowered and sharply replied, "You mean an abortion?"

Embarrassed, she said, "Um, no, I meant there must be something I can take since it is so early in the pregnancy."

"Absolutely not. That is not allowed, and neither are abortions."

"But what if I can't do it?"

"Listen, Mrs. Lopez, you have no options but to go ahead with the pregnancy," the doctor said impatiently.

"Well, is there something you can give me to avoid future pregnancies, now that I will have four small children so close together in age?"

Shaking his head, the doctor said, "You should be happy."

Connie could no longer prevent the tears from spilling over, brushing them away as she attempted to keep her gown closed. The doctor watched her but gave no indication of sympathy or understanding. She prayed to herself, *what next?*

"I will leave you a prescription for pre-natal pills at the desk," he said, leaving the exam room without a backward glance.

Stunned and upset, Connie's tears soon turned into sobs. A nurse knocked on the door and said they were waiting for the room and then asked quietly, "Are you all right?" Not responding to the query, Connie dressed, trying to dry her tears by tearing off paper liner from the exam table. She dashed to the front desk, grabbed the prescription, and left without saying goodbye to the receptionist. Balling up the prescription, she tossed it into her purse.

Connie stumbled onto the street corner to wait for the No. 92 bus. The hot sun beating down on her did little to cheer her up. She felt better when she saw there were no other riders at the bus station. Connie was not presentable at the moment, nor was she in the mood to indulge in polite hellos, much less have conversations with strangers. She had a long wait until the next bus. *What am I going to do? What am I going to do? Oh, dear God, what am I going to do?* The question kept playing like a tune she could not extricate from her mind.

Connie knew she had to do something. But, what? Connie knew nothing about such things. This topic was never discussed in her childhood home. At work, she had heard murmurings about various methods women used to perform abortions—different herbs, the use of sharp implements, the application of abdominal pressure and other techniques, all of which had been used for a long time.

Legalized abortion would not come until much later, when in 1973 the United States Supreme Court ruled that women have a right to privacy under the 14th Amendment. This would be a public-health triumph for pregnant women that ranked with awareness of antisepsis and antibiotics.

However, in 1949, few doctors would perform abortions, as it meant risking their medical licenses. Women who could afford to pay a high price could find private abortions, but Connie did not have that kind of

94

money, nor did she know where to find such a doctor. Women—particularly women like Connie—had to figure it out on their own or with the assistance of other women.

Connie had heard that there were certain drinks one could take that would induce a miscarriage. Could she do it? She knew there were other more drastic things one could do that included inserting objects into her vagina, but Connie didn't have the nerve to hurt herself. Some women said jumping up and down would help. Surely, she could do that, but she was not sure it worked.

Connie cried all the way home. People on the bus looked the other way as they passed her seat, pretending not to notice the tears rolling down her cheeks or her obvious distress. One kind elderly woman handed her a tissue as she passed by, but continued walking down the aisle to a seat in the back of the bus.

She would have to tell Oscar about the pregnancy. She would tell him she did not want the baby. Could she tell him she wanted to end this pregnancy? Probably not since he seemed so overjoyed by all her other pregnancies. She had to come up with a plan because she could not risk another pregnancy.

Religious from an early age, Connie attended church every Sunday and some weekdays whenever she could. She knew the Roman Catholic Church's views on marriage, sin, and abortions. She genuinely believed these teachings, but remained naive about how the Church came to its doctrines on issues affecting women's bodies. The Church was against abortion, no matter the circumstances, maintaining that all abortions were a sin. Such dogmatic edicts created serious dilemmas for many young couples. Should they follow the dictates of the Church or be condemned to hell? Should they have a baby they could not afford or did not want? True believers were faced with difficult choices.

In the 1940s, the Church advised Catholic women to use the rhythm method to prevent pregnancies. It banned all other contraception practices. The Church knew of the rhythm method's ineffectiveness, but it was all they offered to desperate women other than abstinence. For mothers who ended up pregnant while using the rhythm method, the church often blamed the couple saying they had not followed the process correctly. The other response proffered by the Church was that it was God's will to have a child and parents should rejoice in creating new life.

Thinking about the baby maturing inside her, Connie was torn between what she had been taught and the actual conditions of her stressful day-to-day existence. Connie recognized that abortion was wrong, that it was a mortal sin, but in her case it was something that had to be done. Terrified of having another baby and equally shocked at her own frantic musings she wondered, *Could I live with myself if I got rid of this child?*

She prayed and prayed for for some guidance on how she should proceed. Tossing and turning she was troubled and unable to sleep at night. She had to do something. *But what?* She kept thinking to herself, *what can I do? What, dear God, is the right thing to do?* There was no one to help or advise her.

CHAPTER 22

Connie knew she had to act soon, but when? Time was running out. The next day she told her employer she had a doctor's appointment. Leaving work early, she headed straight for the library to see what information she could gather. She had copied down a word she thought might help, but she did not know what it meant or even how to pronounce it. Someone had told her that was the solution. The word was abortifacient. Her first stop, after speaking with the reference desk, was to find out what it meant and how it could help her.

The reference elderly librarian looked up, smiled and asked Connie, "How can I help you?"

Connie felt tongue-tied but knew she had to say her request aloud. Connie looked down as she murmured, "I am looking for books with information on contraception."

Abruptly, the friendly librarian's demeanor changed and with a disapproving stare she said, "Well, we don't have much, and the books are on another floor. Did you want me to get you the couple of books we have? I will need to hold your library card while you review them since they are available here only for reference."

Connie nodded, reluctantly handing over her card. She did not want the librarian to hold her card. It had her name and all her information on it, but she had no choice. The librarian returned with two small books and handed them to Connie, reminding her that they must be returned to her. She made her way to the large room where she found the large Webster's Dictionary on a wooden pedestal. Rumbling about in her purse, she located the piece of paper with the word she had to look up, as she knew she would not remember how to spell the word from memory. Making herself comfortable in a chair near the dictionary, she flipped through the pages looking for the word.

Finding it, she learned that abortifacients were powerful herbs. Connie picked up one of books she had on contraception and looked up the word. It stated that abortifacients should only be used for short periods of time, were hard on the body and could stress the kidneys and liver. The book listed countless herbs, along with warnings on toxicity, emphasizing they were unsafe if used regularly. The book cautioned that the sooner these remedies were used, the more likely one would accomplish their goal. "Herbs," the text said, "seem to be effective through the fourth week." The book explicitly stated it was not advisable to begin any herbal treatment after the sixth week of pregnancy. Connie was four weeks pregnant.

Connie scanned the lengthy list of herbs—Angelica, Black Cohosh, Blue Cohosh, Cotton Root Bark, Evening Primrose, Parsley, Pennyroyal, Tansy, Vitamin C, and Pineapple (unripe). Many were toxic while others like Vitamin C had to be used before the fifth week of pregnancy. She was not familiar with any of them other than Vitamin C.

The chapter on "Other Options" recommended hot baths, jogging, and jumping rope, along with drinking herbal teas. Other suggestions included long car rides or train rides. Connie found one idea shocking—having an orgasm during sex. According to the reference book, "The motion of sex relaxes the pelvic muscles, and the orgasm helps the uterus contract 'loosening' up a tight cervix, which aids in releasing the fetus. Some women reported favorable results when they had orgasms combined with the use of herbs."

Connie wasn't sure about any of this. Had she had an orgasm? How did you make sure you had one? She was sure she had not had one, but she didn't know enough about it. Besides, if that was true, it seems ridding oneself of a fetus would be a lot simpler. It was all too confusing and scandalous to contemplate, and it seemed to mix up pleasure with destruction. This was more than Connie could wrap her mind around. She did not want to put these two opposites together. This was not something she wanted to think about.

Taking quick notes, Connie returned the reference books to the librarian who handed her library card back. Still embarrassed by their earlier encounter, Connie gave the librarian a rushed 'thank you' on exiting the library. Her mind was reeling all the way home. She did not know which herbs would be best. There were so many, it was so confusing, and some were exceptionally toxic. Also, she would have to attempt the abortion when Oscar was not home, maybe when he was working overtime.

Should she tell someone? Was there someone she could trust? Connie decided she could not jeopardize her plan by sharing this information with anyone. She was entirely on her own. The thought terrified her. *What if something went wrong?*

While she reviewed which were the choicest and safest herbs, her conscience kicked up a storm. *It is a mortal sin to abort a fetus.* This mantra kept repeating itself over and over. She tried to disregard the little voice in her head that also kept saying, *it's wrong, it's wrong.* Arguing with herself, she kept encouraging herself, saying *I have to do it.* Ignoring the echoing noises, she reminded herself she needed to have her wits about her. Having another child would not be good for the ones she already had. Then, to stop the incessant chatter in her head, Connie started heavy duty praying for guidance, begging her favorite saints for advice and courage. *And,* she breathed, *please make sure the tincture works.*

In the end, Connie utilized cotton root bark. Her notes revealed that cotton root bark proved to be the most effective abortifacient because it contained all the necessary elements to halt a pregnancy. The book explained how cotton root bark interrupted a pregnancy. It seemed out of her realm of general knowledge about her body, but Connie knew she had to understand how it worked if she was going to do it. She was not convinced she understood any of it after studying her notes.

The pharmacist at her local drug store told her there was a small herbal shop on the outer edge of Tucson that sold it. She had hinted to the pharmacist she wanted to purchase herbs to lose weight so he would not be suspicious. *Perhaps the workers at the herbal shop can give me more information on how to use the cotton root bark,* she hoped. Physically getting to the herbal shop would be a challenge without a car, but she would figure it out. The mere mechanics of getting to the distant location was overwhelming. Connie had to consider how long she could leave the kids alone, public transportation to the shop, securing the needed information and racing back to the kids as soon as possible. With effort, Connie worked out a schedule, the bus line and made her way to the herbalist shop.

An elderly Asian man stood near a side door as she entered. She asked him if he had cotton root bark.

"Yes, I have some," he responded.

"I'd like to purchase some," Connie said softly. "I do not know how to use it. Can you please tell me what I need to do?"

The man explained as plainly as he could.

"You will need to make a tincture from the cotton root bark. First, you must carefully peel the bark off the root, cut it into pieces, then boil it in a quart of water until the water turns brown and it is reduced by half. Then, you must put twelve teaspoons of this tincture into every quart of water that you drink."

Looking puzzled, Connie asked, "How difficult is it to scrape the bark off the root? Is there an easy way to remove it?"

"No easy way," the herbalist responded. "Use a sharp knife. You must drink one to two quarts of this tea per day, then take ten drops of tincture every two hours until bleeding is underway."

Still unsure, Connie asked him to repeat the instructions again making a deliberate effort to concentrate and remember every word he said. She was not positive she could drink that much tea in a single day, and she worried about the taste.

"How does it taste once it's made?" she asked concerned.

"Don't know how it tastes. Never tasted it," he said grimacing.

Searching his face, Connie asked her most pressing question, "Does it work?"

"No complaints. Have return customers," he said.

Paying the herbalist for the cotton root bark and satisfied she had all the instructions, Connie rushed to catch the bus and return home to her children.

Connie waited a couple of days before trying to make the formula. The dark brown bark was surprisingly rough and uneven to the touch and grazed her as she held it in her hand. Using her sharpest knife, she scraped and scraped to get to the root disconnected from the bark. A musty, earthy smell emanated from the root. It was hard work to get it all off evenly and her hands had deep scratches from the jagged edges jutting out on the craggy bark. Holding the root in her hands, Connie set about making the tincture as the herbalist had instructed and measuring it carefully into a quart of water.

Setting it on the table, Connie sat down and stared at it. Dark and muddy looking, it would be a lot to drink. The little voice inside her started acting up again. She had just raised the tea to her lips when Connie heard a loud scream from one of her daughters. She ran into the other room to discover her older daughter pulling Christina's hair with all her might while holding her down on the floor. The younger child was screaming her head off as she tried to escape from her sister. Pulling her eldest daughter off her sister, Connie admonished her and sent them both their separate ways, returning to the kitchen determined to take the first sip of tea before any other interruptions occurred.

The taste amazed her. It was not good, but it was not as horrible as she had expected. Perhaps she could do this. She took another mouthful, then sat back and reflected on what she was doing. She stared at the full bottle of formula sitting on the table in front of her. *Yes, it bothered her, but I have no choice,* she told herself. She drank the first quart slowly, but managed to finish it.

Connie carefully hid the rest of the tincture in the back of the cupboards behind the flour and sugar packages and went to check on the kids. Connie would take more later. Curiously she felt nothing, not that she thought she would in the beginning. She continued drinking the tea for the next three days.

Everything seemed to be going along when she started to feel sick, very sick. She did not know if it was from the tincture or from something else. Connie was healthy, but this change disturbed her. Should she stop?

Not sure what to do, she returned to the herbalist's shop and asked him if the tea could cause her illness. He listened carefully as she relayed her symptoms. He scratched his head and said he didn't know and that maybe she should stop. But, he added, it was up to her. He knew it worked, or at least that is what they had told him.

Distraught and unsure what to do, Connie stopped taking the tea. It scared her and she was afraid of becoming deathly ill. She did not want to leave her children without a mother, and no one would know why she had become ill. With no one to talk to about her dilemma, and despite no longer taking the abortifacient, she was having misgivings about her actions. *Have I committed a mortal sin by trying to kill my baby? Was it still a sin because it was my intent, even though I didn't not go through with it?* The mortal sin part was not the most compelling reason she stopped. *Did that mean I am going to hell and that I'm not a good mother?*

With no one to share her fears and physical pain, she ruefully told Oscar what she had done. At first Oscar appeared shaken, then he asked her why. Connie tried to explain that the pregnancies were too close together and the doctor would not help her. She did not know what else to do. Oscar became livid. He told her that all children were wanted and that things would work out. Why didn't she believe that? Connie saw that Oscar believed what he was saying, but she did not think it would be all right. She did not believe having another baby would improve things and she secretly feared it might make her circumstances worse.

Tears streamed down Connie's face as she headed to the bedroom. The next day, Connie threw out the rest of the formula.

CHAPTER 23

Connie's second son, Daniel, was born on Christmas Eve, December 23, 1949. A healthy baby boy with a full head of hair, he soon became one of Connie's favorites. Oscar was euphoric with the birth of a second son. He told her they had enough money to make the move to the new house in Pueblo Gardens. Connie was impatient to live in a house big enough to hold the entire family. She had seen the sunny bright house, and she was expecting the additional space would resolve issues between her and Oscar, like keeping a neater house for one, and giving the children a safe outdoors place to run and play. It would mean less fighting among them and a more peaceful environment for her and the family.

In her honest moments, Connie knew that the problems between her and Oscar were greater than a location or physical space. Oscar loved to argue as a form of communication. In fact, argument was one of Oscar's favorite forms of discourse and the one he used exclusively. He did it to prove his intelligence.

In contrast, Connie was a peacemaker at heart and liked no form of disagreement, much less argument. This made for unpleasant encounters between them. Connie's general response to Oscar's communication style was to shrug and not respond, which angered him. To avoid serious problems, Connie would leave the room. As soon as the kids grew older, Oscar's penchant for this type of communication was extended to them. Sometimes Oscar would take outrageous positions to get the kids riled up or attempt to get them into political debates. He often left the house angry if the debate had not gone his way.

Oscar's oldest daughter stopped getting hooked when she understood the game. It saddened her that Oscar's primary means (and often his only way) of connecting with his kids and Connie was limited to this disruptive and often slighting method. She wished he understood that there were many other modes of communication and that he did not have to prove his intelligence by provoking arguments with his family.

In the spring of 1950, the Lopez family moved into their long-awaited home. It thrilled the kids, and Oscar was delighted to be moving into a brand-new place. After depositing all their belongings in the house, the family discovered they needed more furniture. New beds, cribs, and a kitchen table with chairs would soon fill the house's empty spaces and add to the comfort of the growing family.

Shortly after moving in, Connie had difficulty managing an even larger house and keeping it tidy, one of Oscar's pet peeves. Connie had not realized that the larger space would need more care and attention until they were in it. Oscar often raved that he wanted a clean house and dinner on the table when he got home from work, no matter what time he arrived. It did not matter that Connie had been busy trying to keep track of the kids, feed them and clean them up so they would look presentable for their dad when he got home.

Cooking for her expanding family was overwhelming. As soon as one meal was completed and eaten, it was time to prepare the next one. Then there were the loads of dishes each meal created. Sometimes Connie just let them pile up. She did not find cooking endless meals and keeping the household running smoothly that rewarding, particularly with limited money to buy food. It was not what she had in mind when she married. She never foresaw so many children, not that she had ever thought far into the future.

Now, she found herself in a position she had never even imagined and with only limited moments to reflect on how she had gotten here. Connie had simply wanted to stay in the United States and have a boyfriend in the beginning. *Something is missing. But what? There must be more to life*, she thought sadly. She had four lovable children, but they were all needy and energetic. Each one had their own distinct personality and desires. Because they were so close in age, they were always running around chasing one another, fighting along the way. She tried to intercede occasionally, but on some days she just sat at the table contemplating her life, and wondered how it had all come to this. The kids did not follow her directions to behave, sometimes ignoring her, unlike Oscar. When he spoke, they minded him immediately.

Then, there was her husband, who seemed to be more distant and more argumentative than ever. She never seemed to do or say anything right according to him. She tried to engage with Oscar on subjects that interested him but did not call to her. He was a baseball fanatic, so Connie listened to games and was surprised how much she enjoyed them. They also shared a love of certain operas and some music, but Connie did not enjoy the Ranchera "musica" that so captivated Oscar.

Connie found Oscar's ideas on women antiquated and chauvinistic. He did not think his views were outdated and would not listen to her thoughts when she tried to explain things were changing. He angered easily on the subject of women and their role in society. Oscar liked to call women "dames," which Connie found insulting. Eventually, Connie learned to keep her thoughts to herself rather than risk his wrath. And she thought, *What difference does it make? He always thinks he is right. Don't argue*, she constantly reminded herself. *It only causes more strife.* So, Connie remained silent most of the time.

The quietest time of the day was at night when the kids were in their beds and cribs. One problem was that her two sons would regularly rock their cribs so roughly they moved them clear across the room, creating tremendous racket as they moved across the hardwood floor. Then, they would throw their glass milk bottles out of the cribs onto the floor, shattering them. The boys did this almost every time they were placed in their cribs. Connie would rush into the room and tell them to stop it. There were many shattered bottles to clean up regularly. Plastic bottles were not yet on the market in those early years.

More often, she would ask her daughters to go into their room and tell "the boys" to stop rocking and banging their cribs. "Tell them to go to sleep," she would say to her daughters. As the two older boys grew, they continued the rocking, later extending this action to the sofa and to the living room chairs, destroying furniture throughout the years.

It would be almost thirty years before Connie's eldest daughter discovered what all the rocking and banging was about. Watching a special television presentation on orphanages in Romania, she saw rows and rows of cribs where the children sat and stood shaking and bashing their cribs, triggering long forgotten memories of her brothers. The news commentator explained that children rocked in their cribs to self-stimulate when they were not receiving enough physical touch, something that was very difficult to achieve in orphanages where there were a few caretakers. It was then that Connie's daughter recognized that her brothers had needed more touch as infants. Connie had no awareness of this need. Understanding that her mother never knew of this deprivation, her daughter did not share this information with Connie.

Connie adored music from an early age and had a lovely singing voice. Before marriage, she sang professionally with her three sisters. All sopranos, they sang on the radio in the early 1940s under the name of the Martinez Sisters. It was fun to reminisce about it. Connie shared stories about the songs they sang on the radio with her children even though those times were now part of her past. She loved singing in church and could be observed walking around her house humming to herself as she cleaned.

In Connie's spare moments, she would chase the children outside to play and then sit down and turn on the radio to listen to Mario Lanza or to an opera. Oscar and Connie shared a love of Mario Lanza, the most famous opera singer in the 1940s and early 1950s. They knew him for his role as Pinkerton in Puccini's Madame Butterfly, Connie's favorite opera. Mario Lanza crossed over to popular music and won an Academy Award for the song "Because You're Mine," a song dear to Connie. Oscar and Connie had his records and would listen to them together every once in a while in the early days before the children.

In April 1951, she received alarming news. She was pregnant, again. Their fifth child would be due in early December. Connie was too shocked to react and did not tell Oscar as she had in the past. She no longer let her mother know about her pregnancies, as she had received no support from her, and Maria had never approved of her having so many children. *As if there were something I could do about it!* Connie fumed.

CHAPTER 24

Oscar was working more and more overtime. Every once in a while, he would stop by to see his childhood friend, Julia, to say hi and see how she was doing. Ever since his return to Tucson, Julia had been angry with him. She had been more than a little surprised to learn that he married in Los Angeles, but then to bring his wife and child back to Tucson was more than she could stand. She never thought Oscar would do this to her. When she had asked him to explain why he had done it, he told her an incredible story about trying to help Connie, so she would not have to leave the country. None of it made sense to her, and to be honest, she did not believe it, anyway.

Julia felt betrayed. Long ago, Oscar had said he would marry her, and he had broken his promise. Julia knew they were meant to be together and that she was better for him than Connie. Not that she knew Connie at all, just from what she knew of her. Oscar had said she was not a great cook or housekeeper. He hinted there were issues with the children. She was not sure what he meant, but she did not think it was good. Oh, how she loved children and birds. She wanted to have his children.

Oscar's visits to Julia's were becoming more frequent. He would stop by for a beer on the way home and they would talk about his work and the children. Julia sensed that all was not well at home but did not ask questions. Still, she was growing more hopeful for a future relationship. She felt bad because she had heard from a friend, not Oscar, that Connie was pregnant again. Julia knew she should stop seeing him, but she could not make herself do it. Then there was her mother, who had asked her what she was doing with a married man, one with four children and a fifth on the way. Julia did not know how to respond.

One day, Julia's mother, Esmeralda, stopped her and said, "Majita, we have to talk about what you are doing. You must stop. It will not end well."

Julia retorted, "Mama, I love him and have always loved him. I cannot live without him. We made a vow to marry when we were young. I know it is wrong, but I have to follow my heart."

Wringing her hands, her mother countered, "You are hurting those children. You must stop this now before it goes too far. Promise me you will not see him again."

"I can't..." Julia cried, despondent. "I don't know what to do. I try to forget him, but when I see him, it starts all over again. I tell myself I must stop, but Mama, I can't do it. I pray for help every day."

Esmeralda looked down so her daughter could not see her face. She, too, had prayed and prayed asking that her daughter would find a better path for her life. She noticed that Julia went to church more often, and that gave her faith her daughter would make the right choice. If only she would meet another man, then she could let Oscar go.

Besides praying for her daughter, Esmeralda did not know what more she could do. She thought about talking to Father Alfonso, the local parish priest, and petitioning him for his prayers and direction for her daughter. Yet she could not get up the nerve to speak to him. He was so outspoken in his approach which frightened Julia's mother, so she had kept her thoughts to herself. Esmeralda was not sure what she could do. She did not want to discuss this with any of her family members either even though many were aware of the situation. She was ashamed of her daughter's behavior and yet she loved Julia and wanted to protect her.

Julia stomped out of the house after her exchange with her mother. On her way down the street, she saw a group of young children playing hopscotch, shouting with glee as they jumped. She noticed they were close in age to Oscar's children. She felt sick to her stomach thinking about her mother's harsh words. They hurt but they were true. She needed to change the direction of her life. She needed to stop seeing Oscar. Just thinking about it cut her to the quick, but her mother was right. Oscar's children needed their father. She would tell Oscar she could no longer see him.

Julia would tell him the next time he stopped by. Oscar did not show up for the next three days. On the fourth day, he arrived and appeared to be his normal, talkative, outgoing self. He went on and on about his job and the children. She listened and handed him a beer with hardly any comment.

Then, Julia took deep breath and said, "Oscar, we need to talk."

Oscar paused and looked at her. "What is it, Julia? Are you sick?"

"Yes, in a way I guess I am," she said. "We cannot continue this way. It is making me sick. I can't keep seeing you under these circumstances. I want us to be together but not like this. I want to end this, Oscar, for me and for you. You need to focus on Connie and your children. Please don't stop by anymore."

Oscar frowned at Julia in disbelief.

"What do you mean?" he asked. "Just like that, you say you don't want to see me? What about my feelings? Don't I have a say in this at all?"

Shaking her head, Julia pushed forth, "No, you want me and your family. You can't have both of us. Go back to Connie and try to make it work."

Angry, Oscar slammed his beer can down dribbling some on the table. He got up and stormed out of Julia's house. She heard his truck pull away on the gravel driveway as it sped towards the street.

Julia sat down and cried. Well, she had done it. It was the hardest thing she had ever done, but she needed to move on with her life. She saw the beer dripping on the floor from the can where Oscar had left it. Julia moved to grab a kitchen towel to mop up the spilled beer before her mother returned. Yes, she had seen her mother leave the house just as Oscar's truck pulled up.

When her mother returned, she found Julia sitting in the kitchen holding a dripping towel in one hand with her head lying across her other arm on the table, sobbing.

"What happened, Julia?" her mother whispered, concerned.

"Well, you should be happy. It's over. That's what you wanted, right?" Julia said, hiccupping through her sobs.

"No, Julia, I wanted you to be happy and have a good life. You were not headed that way with Oscar. You can find another man. There are other men, you know," her mother said, knowing that Julia was not listening to her anymore.

"Not like Oscar. I don't want to talk about it anymore. You wanted it ended. Let it go, Mama. Leave me alone, please." Her mother retreated from the kitchen, leaving Julia weeping.

Oscar fumed as he drove home. How dare Julia tell him to get lost. *No one treats me that way, not even Julia,* he mumbled to himself as he steered the car. Getting angrier by the minute, he stepped on the gas, almost hitting the slow-moving car in front of him. Banging on his horn, he gave the driver the finger and continued on home.

CHAPTER 25

Oscar looked aggravated when he arrived home, which alerted Connie to avoid him as much as possible. The kids were running around like maniacs, so Connie sent them outside to play. Actually, she was not feeling that well herself. She was in her seventh month, so getting around was difficult. Having gained over 30 pounds, all Connie wanted to do was sit down and put her feet up. But that was not possible; she had to get dinner on the table. Oscar glared at her as she crossed his path. Connie pretended not to notice. She was getting superb at not noticing a lot of things. Besides she had done nothing, but that did not seem to matter to her husband.

By the next day, Oscar seemed calmer as he left for work. Connie, meanwhile, was depressed. It was difficult getting around and trying to keep the house in order and meals on the table. She was exerting every ounce of energy she possessed taking care of the household. She did not think Oscar noticed or appreciated it and the kids' main refrain was, "I'm hungry. When are we going to eat?"

Oscar was home more now, which was both good and bad. He complained if the house was not in good order and never seemed entirely pleased with the food no matter how hard she tried. Connie had spoken to her mother twice in the last month and only recently told her the baby was due the first week of December. Her mother did not say much, but Connie could hear the disapproval in her voice when she asked if it was to be the last one. What could she say?

Things fell into a routine. Oscar seemed to settle down. He spent more time at home and often had his brother Manny and his family over for dinner. They would take the kids to Lilia's for a meal. Lilia was such a good cook that Connie loved to go there, but not just for the food. She loved the support that Lilia gave her. With few friends in Tucson, she still missed Los Angeles. Tucson was much quieter and hotter and she did not like the thunderstorms common in the summer months when sunshine turned quickly to grey dark skies, thunder roared loudly, and rain splattered on the dry sidewalks and streets scenting the air. The kids loved the sudden thunderstorms. They would run outside as soon as the storm stopped, splashing with abandon in the flooded streets, jumping up and down screaming with joy. One time, a local reporter caught sight of the children playing in the water after a heavy rainstorm and he took their picture. It appeared in the next day's newspaper to the kids' absolute delight.

The kids begged and begged for a dog, and so they added a cocker spaniel to the Lopez household. To Connie, it meant one more thing to care for, but the children loved the animal, so Connie agreed to keep it. Money continued to be an issue, but she was looking forward to having the baby and moving on.

A baby boy named Lawrence arrived on December 10, 1951. Larry had a few tufts of hair sticking up and came into the world with one loud squeal. Connie felt her family was now complete. She had five kids: a five-year-old, a four-year-old, a three-year-old, a two-year-old, and a newborn. That was a lot for anyone but for Connie at 30 years old, it was an extraordinary number of children. She made peace with it and continued to do her best. *If only Oscar would be more empathetic*, she thought to herself, *life would be so much easier.*

Oscar was very proud of his brood. It was what he had always wanted—a family of his own to love and cherish. He should be happy. That is what he told himself. And he was. It was just that things were not what he wanted between Connie and him. Even though he lacked the words to articulate the problem, he knew they were not an even match. He liked to argue, cook, enjoy the children, and spend money. Connie had little patience for these things. He liked her but was not sure he could say he loved her.

Julia spoke to his soul in a way that no other woman did. They connected so long ago, saw things in similar ways. Julia loved to cook, loved children, and loved to mother him, or to use Oscar's own words, "take care of him in ways he never experienced as a child." This need to be nurtured was something missing in Oscar's life, something he yearned for at a profound level, even though he was not conscious of it. Connie did not "mother" him. She never knew that this was something he desperately craved. Connie was not a woman with the time or resources to do a lot of internal contemplating and speculating about her or her husband's motivations. Connie needed a husband to take care of her.

Oscar continued to work hard and keep his nose clean. He avoided Julia's part of town and no longer saw her. Oscar thought about her and heard about her through friends and family who were in contact with her. Recently, he learned she was going out with one man and that it was serious. *That is no longer my business*, he told himself. Oscar had to admit it bothered him. Though he tried to be more committed to his marriage, he continued to be distracted. Oscar saw that Connie was having a tough time with the kids and knew he should help her more and stop being so critical, but Oscar could not seem to stop himself. It was not fair to her and he knew it.

CHAPTER 26

In late 1952, Oscar and Connie sent their eldest daughter, who was seven years old, to Los Angeles to attend school there and live with her grandmother. They gave no explanations to her or her siblings other than she would be going to Los Angeles for the school year. Years later, neither Connie nor Oscar could explain why the decision was made to send their firstborn away. Perhaps Oscar felt it would take pressure off Connie.

For the eldest daughter, who would be in the second grade, the change in her home environment would be drastic. Siblings would no longer surround her. Instead, she would live with her grandmother who spoke only Spanish. More frightening to Connie's eldest daughter was discovering her grandmother's enduring disapproval of her, her siblings, and her father. It would be a tough year for the little girl since her grandmother had firm ideas on how to raise children, having had nine herself.

Of all of Connie's children, her eldest daughter would be the child who spent the most time with Maria and who would come to know her best. It was a trying time for the young girl who was not fluent in Spanish. For the year she lived with her grandmother, many issues would arise, from the amount and types of food she ate, to limits on friends and television, to being required to work in her grandmother's candle factory after school preparing candles for sale.

One tumultuous issue between the young child and Maria concerned her persistence on teaching her granddaughter how to sew. Maria insisted on teaching her granddaughter on a large industrial sewing machine she loved and used so well. In fairness, not only was the machine very large, it ran quickly, especially for a seven-year-old child's motor skills. But speed was not what troubled the child most. The child could not abide by the use of mixed unmatched colors on a garment and refused to sew. Maria said it did not matter. It took too much time to change the thread each time.

This became a major contention between them with Maria complaining to Connie about her daughter's food habits and her refusal to sew. Connie did not know what to say or do as she knew her mother and her daughter well. *Both*, she thought to herself, *could be stubborn and unyielding.* So, she would change the subject whenever her mother brought it up. Eventually to end the complaints, Connie told her mother her daughter did not need to learn to sew.

The seven-year-old was fully conscious of Maria's strong will and her intent to bend her to that will. She observed her aunts and uncles and saw how they were afraid to cross their mother or express their opinion if it differed from Maria's. Somehow the girl determined she would not be like her mother, her aunts, or even her uncles. The young girl never allowed her grandmother to frighten her or overrule her. She was, she believed, perhaps naively, in charge of herself even though she was only seven years old. There remained years of quiet acquiescence between the granddaughter and grandmother. That unspoken understanding continued to exist when her granddaughter would again live with her during her high school years.

By 1954, money had gotten tighter and tighter and Oscar and Connie argued about it constantly. Tension in the house was high. Oscar did not want to restrain his spending. Connie advised him they had to be more careful with their money. Feeding and clothing five children was costly, and expenses kept creeping higher and higher. Connie had an astute understanding of how to manage money and how to save it. This was something Oscar neither knew or cared about. Oscar saw money as a vehicle for gaining items he desired for himself or his family. He always thought it would work out and there was no need to worry like Connie did. Her constant badgering about money irritated Oscar, who continued to be blasé about finances saying, "It would work out somehow."

Connie knew better. They were on a road to disaster if they did not get their finances in order. They would have to move out of Pueblo Gardens. Connie spent many nights worrying about money shortages while Oscar snored contentedly at her side. He seemed oblivious to the upcoming financial storm.

As the Lopez family rang in 1955, things were not looking good for them. Finances were in a crisis and they were having trouble making house payments. The fighting continued, and her eldest daughter would hear her mother crying softly at night occasionally. Oscar felt he was being nagged about money all the time and he could not stand it.

He would drive by Julia's street hoping to catch a glimpse of her. Oscar had not seen her in a while, and felt he needed to see her. Fighting an internal battle over whether he should just show up at her door, he knew if he did, she would see him. He was concerned about Julia's mom, who always made a face whenever she observed him. He saw judgment in it, and he did not like it.

Finally, he could stand it no more. Oscar needed to see and talk to someone who understood him and that someone was Julia. He knew she would be irritated by him showing up unexpectedly, but he was hoping to win her over by telling her that things were not working out with Connie.

Oscar told himself he should try harder with Connie, but they did not agree on anything. She did not know or understand him, particularly not how he liked things done like Julia did. It was Julia he needed, so he decided he would stop by the next day on the way home from work.

The next day, Oscar headed down Julia's street. He parked his white truck two houses away from her residence hoping that her mother would not see him, and she was not home. He took a deep breath as he rang the bell. Her mother opened the door and her annoyance was plainly visible.

"I need to see Julia," Oscar blurted.

"She's not home from work yet," she stammered. "What are you doing here, anyway? I thought she was finished with you. Have you no shame? A married man with five children. What do you want with my daughter? Can't you leave her alone? Please, Oscar, I am begging you to go away and leave her alone, so she can move on with her life."

Oscar stared at Julia's mother for a full moment. For once in his life, he was at a loss of words. What she said was true, but he still needed Julia.

He looked down and then lifting his eyes and glaring at Esmeralda he forcefully said, "Dammit, I don't need your permission to see your daughter. She is an adult and can see whoever she wants. I'll wait outside in my truck and never talk that way to me again."

Fuming, he marched to his truck, moving it so it was parked directly in front of Julia's mother's house. *The hell with her*, he thought. *I'll do as I damn well please.* Sitting in his truck, he fiddled with the radio to see if he could catch a game. No such luck, so he put music on and waited. An hour elapsed before Julia drove up. She seemed distracted as she climbed out of her vehicle. She did not notice him sitting in the truck. As she headed up the walkway, he tapped on his horn to get her attention. She looked up surprised to see Oscar. She headed back towards the truck, opened the passenger door, and slid into the front seat next to him.

"Did my mother see you?" she asked worriedly.

"Yes, and she gave me hell and told me to get lost."

"What did you tell her?"

"That you were an adult and could do and see whoever you wanted without her permission."

"Oscar, what do you want? It's been a while, and I've moved on with my life. But you already know that, right?"

"Yes. But, Julia, I need you. I've missed you and our talks. Things are not good at home and I had to see you again."

Julia's face turned ashen. "Oscar, you know I am seeing someone. He's a nice guy and he has no children," Julia said defiantly. "What is it you want from me? You are married, and it looks like you are staying that way."

"You're wrong, Julia. I have been thinking about it for a long time and it's not working out. I will leave Connie. I need to work out the details. You know it's complicated."

What Oscar didn't tell her was that he was in financial trouble, and that the family would have to move. He asked Julia if she still loved him. She turned her back to him as she decided how she wanted to respond. Did he not know she had never stopped loving him?

"Oscar, I don't know what you want me to say. Will saying I still love you change anything? Look, you know how I feel about you now and have always felt. That will not change, but I can't keep waiting around for you."

"Look, Julia, if you give me one more chance. I promise we'll be together."

Julia gazed into Oscar's eyes and saw he meant what he said. It made her sad though, since it meant breaking up a family, and she would be the responsible party. Julia's heart melted at the thought of being with Oscar. She asked him if he wanted to come and have a beer.

"What about your mother?" he asked.

"If we are going to be together, she might as well know as soon as possible. I am not saying she will be happy. She won't be, but it is my home, too. Let's go in."

Hesitantly, he followed her up the walkway. As they walked in, her mother scowled and left the kitchen for her room slamming the door behind her.

Julia said, "She'll get over it. Ignore her now. I am so glad to see you."

Over the next couple of months, Oscar stopped by whenever he could. He noticed her mother made herself scarce during his visits. She never answered the door. When he asked Julia how her mother was taking it, she shrugged her shoulders and said, "The same way she took it the last time we were together. Don't worry about it."

Oscar was not sure why, but he worried. Julia's mother made him nervous. And things at home had only gotten worse.

CHAPTER 27

On evenings when Oscar was not around, Connie lay in bed trying to muffle her crying from the children. She would lock the bedroom door and tell the children she had a headache. Meanwhile, the dishes continued to pile high in the sink while the kids ran in and out of the house with uncontrolled frivolity oblivious of their mother's deepening pain. Oscar tried to refrain from criticizing, but often lost patience with Connie berating her shortcomings as a wife and mother.

Nothing wounded Connie more than Oscar continually pointing out her shortcomings. She knew them all. Bringing them up made her feel worse. She had tried so hard. There were too many kids and though she loved them, it took all her strength to keep going. She felt Oscar distancing himself from her more and more. Then, there were the money problems that grew more ominous each day.

Now, no matter how scrupulous Connie budgeted, there was not enough money to cover their costs. She did not understand how it would all end, but she knew making the mortgage on Pueblo Gardens was no longer workable and that they would have to move if something did not change. Money problems troubled Connie tremendously and added to her other worries about her marriage.

Oscar and Julia were soon back to their old pattern of visiting. He would stop by for a beer, to talk and sometimes for more several times a week when he could squeeze it in. It must have happened in March of that year. Not sure of the exact date, Julia soon learned she was pregnant. Julia had always been on the Ruben-esque side of womanhood, so she could keep her pregnancy hidden from her mother for an extra couple of months, but by May, she could no longer hide her weight gain even with the extra-large pants she had purchased. Her mother knew her secret.

When confronted by her mother, Julia said, "It's okay, Mom. He'll marry me. He promised."

Her mother's face registered exquisite pain as she looked at the daughter she loved. How did a mother protect her child when the child refused to believe that life might not happen as she hoped? What could she say to her to help her comprehend the enormity of the situation? It seemed impossible to get through to Julia. Convinced Oscar was her childhood sweetheart; Julia would not let the dream go. How would she manage raising a daughter alone? Julia's mother did not think Oscar would leave his wife and five children. Did he even care for Julia? Who knew?

The next couple of months were rocky as Julia had trouble with the pregnancy. Elated about the baby and sure Oscar would help support her until he could get free from his marriage, Julia would not listen to her mother or any of the other naysayers. Their daughter was born in November 1955. There was a lot of gossip since Julia was not married, but she did not care. She ignored it. She loved her daughter fiercely from the day she first held her. Oscar seemed fond of her and happy about her birth even though it complicated his life further. Even her mother, who was very unhappy with the situation, wanted to take care of her baby. Julia was in heaven. She believed it was all going to work out somehow.

Connie remained completely unaware of the situation, though certain relatives of Oscar's, like Lilia, knew what was going on. They did not tell Connie because she seemed so unhappy with her situation. They did not want to burden her further. Also, they were terrified of what Oscar would do if he found out who had told his wife. So those in the know remained silent and watched from the sidelines.

Oscar's eldest daughter was nine years old at the time of her half-sister's birth. She would later learn of the "other family" through overheard conversations and through certain things her mother told her. Julia's eldest daughter would not learn of the existence of the "first family" until she was almost 14 years old.

She would learn about it in a shocking way. Oscar's eldest daughter by Connie would call often asking to speak to Oscar. She never identified who she was but always gave her first name. One day, frustrated and nosey, Julia's eldest daughter asked her dad who was the girl who was always calling and asking to speak to him.

He startled her by saying, "She's your sister."

Oscar explained that she also had two half-sisters and three half-brothers from his marriage to Connie. Many, many years would elapse before all the twelve children would meet face to face. Even then, some truths were held back, and it would take over fifty years before all the facts surrounding their parents' marriages and relationships would be revealed to all the children. One of the most important secrets concerned keeping Julia from ever finding out about Oscar's sixth child with Connie, a daughter who was born three months prior to the birth of Julia's first son. There was a concerted effort to keep Julia from ever learning this truth. On one occasion when Christina and Yolanda were visiting Oscar in Tucson, Julia bragged that she had more children than Connie. Christina immediately started to correct her when Yolanda elbowed her to keep silent. It was clear Julia did not know about the last child. This concealment continued even after her death.

Though excited about her new grandchild, Julia's mother continued to give her a tough time about her status quo, warning her it would not end well. Julia ignored her mother's repeated harangues, focusing on the baby and her needs. She held on tight to the hope that fate was on her side and that love would win out.

Oscar sat Connie down telling her he needed to talk to her about moving out of Pueblo Gardens. He had been looking around and had found a house on Grand Avenue near downtown Tucson. It would cost less money and was large enough for the kids. The second part of his plan was to move in and then tell Connie he wanted a divorce. He felt it was best to first discuss the moving part since that would be hard enough and hold off mentioning the divorce until they were settled in the new place.

Oscar thought Connie would be angry about having to move but she had known for a while it was coming since Oscar had continued to spend more money than he made. It surprised her they had stayed as long as they had. She was glad. She had liked the house, but she was never too crazy about the Pueblo Gardens complex itself. The neighbors were not friendly. It seemed they did not approve of large families. Most had one or two or three kids, not five. It was time to move on. When Oscar told Connie, she nodded her head in acknowledgment and said nothing. At the time, Connie had no idea that Oscar's other relationship was putting an additional financial strain on them.

Two months later, they moved and got established in their new home on Grand Avenue. The kids fancied the new residence because it bordered the Santa Catalina mountains and there was no fence in the front or back yard to obstruct their movements. With space to run around and play and the desert mountain environment providing the additional attraction of snakes, scorpions, and tarantulas in their own backyard, the kids reveled in their new household. Warily, Connie settled in, but it was as though she knew something was amiss. In fact, after they moved in, she discovered she was pregnant again. This time Connie did not tell Oscar right away. What was the point? She knew his feelings about having children.

Still, she knew things were not right between them. He hardly spoke to her most of the time and was away a lot. She was at a loss as what to do to make things better. It seemed she could do nothing to please him and then there were the kids who needed constant attention. Connie found it hard to function and, on some mornings she had to force herself out of bed.

Connie felt certain she could not manage any more children. She knew she had to tell Oscar, but she did not have the will or the heart to do it, so she said nothing, and she continued to drag herself around as best as she could, often crying herself to sleep.

CHAPTER 28

One day Connie received a strange phone message from a woman she did not know. Connie had taken down the phone number but was undecided on whether to return the call or not. It might be about a bill. Connie was about to throw the paper away when she thought, *Well, if it is about a bill, I might as well find out now, rather than later. I'd better call her,* she thought distractedly to herself. She sat down in the kitchen and dialed the number.

A woman answered and said she wanted to talk to Connie. Surprised and puzzled, Connie wondered how the woman knew her name. Perhaps, she thought, it might have been on some bill next to Oscar's name. The woman asked her if she was sitting down. Alarmed by the question, Connie replied she was instantly wondering if the woman knew she was pregnant. She had told no one, and she had not yet put on too much weight. She waited for the woman to speak.

"Connie, my name is Esmeralda. You do not know me. I am calling you to talk to you about my daughter and your husband."

Connie gasped. *What was she talking about?*

"My daughter has been in love with your husband since she was a young girl and they made silly vows back then to marry when they grew up. Your husband went off to the war and then came back to Tucson with you and a child. This was very hard on my daughter. She always thought she would marry him, and she couldn't give up that dream. Believe me, I tried to get her to let him go. I told her he had five children and did everything I could to stop her. She wouldn't listen to me. She kept on seeing your husband."

"Finally, I could bear it no longer. She would go to church with your husband and her daughter. The scandal this caused still did not stop her. So, I spoke to the parish priest there and he asked them not to come back to his church until they straightened out their lives and the mess they were making. In fact, he escorted them out of the church. Connie, I have never been as ashamed of my daughter as I was that Sunday."

"I am sorry to have to tell you all this. I know it is shocking, but you need to know what your husband and my daughter have been up to. Her daughter is almost a year old. I asked her to move out of my house as I could no longer tolerate the situation and told her I would call you and tell you everything. I don't think she believed me, but you had to know what was going on."

There was a pause, and Esmeralda apologized again for calling with such terrible news and hung up.

Connie sat in her chair, stunned. She had never guessed this was going on. Oscar had a child with another woman, and she was pregnant. What was she going to do? A sob escaped and then she glanced at the clock. The kids would be home by 3:30 PM. She knew she had to pull herself together before they got home. But she couldn't do anything but sit there dazed.

The next thing she knew she heard the front door opening. The kids were home from school. Excited and running, they flew into the kitchen, but when they saw their mother's face, they came to a complete halt and gaped at her.

"What's wrong, mommy?" they called out worriedly. Connie glanced at her children and took a deep breath.

"Oh," she said, "I heard some sad news."

"What?" they asked staring at their mother's tear-stained face.

"Grown-up stuff. Why don't you guys go outside in the backyard and play? I'll make you a snack."

The kids hesitated for a moment and then ran out the door screaming. Connie watched them thinking, *What am I going to do now? It did explain a lot of things, though, how Oscar had been acting. How*, she wondered, *had it all gone so wrong?* She wished there was someone she could talk to, but again there was no one.

It was then, too, that she realized everyone had known but her and no one had told her. She could not even imagine what courage it had taken for Esmeralda to call her or was it revenge against her own daughter? Connie doubted it was the latter. The mother must have been so frustrated with the situation and so disapproving that she felt she had to act. What difference did her motivation make, anyway? It was done. Connie now knew what was going on and she had to decide what to do. She still had not told Oscar she was pregnant. That would make a terrible situation worse.

Suddenly, Connie realized she had promised the kids a snack. Searching for something to make that was quick and easy, she could not find anything. She had hidden the cookies and fruit for the kids' school lunches. The kids were quick to find stuff and raid her hideouts, leaving anything extra missing. She felt so alone, and yet she had to keep going. She knew the kids loved applesauce muffins, so she pulled out the flour and other ingredients and started making the muffins. It served as a temporary distraction from her worries. But the tears kept flowing down her cheeks as she stirred the eggs into the sugar and added the dry ingredients.

Connie had to talk to Oscar when he came home. It would be quite a scene and she did not want the kids to hear it. She would have to wait until they went to sleep. She knew Oscar would be furious even though he had no right to be. Connie was the one who had been betrayed.

A short while later, the kids came tearing into the house asking for the snack.

"Not ready," she said.

They smiled at her because even though they were not ready, they caught a whiff of the applesauce muffins baking in the oven. The children loved her muffins. Connie did not make them often, so it was a treat when she did. They looked at her as she busied herself in the kitchen getting dinner ready. She seemed the same and yet something was different about her. What, they could not say, and being kids, they soon became distracted with their own activities, forgetting all about their mother and the earlier scene in the kitchen.

Connie had just gotten dinner on the table when Oscar walked in. He seemed in better humor than usual. *That will change,* Connie thought to herself, *after we talk later, and he finds out I know that he had another child and when he discovers that I am pregnant again.* Dinner was the usual noisy event with the kids talking all at once about school and their friends. Oscar smiled as he watched them. He knew he had to talk to Connie about the divorce. Maybe he would do it tonight.

Oscar had seen Julia earlier in the afternoon and she was pressuring him to get a divorce. Julia wanted to get married as soon as possible, ever since her mother had kicked her out of her house. She was not comfortable living alone in her small apartment with her daughter. Still, it gave her more privacy when Oscar visited, and they did not have to watch Julia's mother leave when he arrived.

She had not seen her mother, but she had heard from her sisters that her mother was angry at her and that she was the one who had gone to talk to the parish priest. She was the reason Oscar and she had been thrown out of the church. It was embarrassing but she would get over it. But she couldn't believe that her own mother had done that to her. That hurt.

Right before dinner, Connie told Oscar that she had to talk to him but wanted to wait until the kids were asleep. *This is so far from where Oscar and I began,* she thought. *And though I love him, I know now it will never work out for so many reasons. But I never thought this is how it would end.*

Since Connie wanted to talk, Oscar had decided that he might as well address the divorce issue head on just like he did everything else. So, when the kids were asleep, and the door was locked, he sat on the bed and looked at Connie before speaking. She had wanted to talk and yet she looked so defeated even though he had not yet uttered one word. He tried not to let that distract him from his mission, which was to tell Connie he wanted a divorce.

"Connie, this is not working," was how he started, but that was not what he had wanted to say.

"I know you are not happy," he said. "Neither am I. We need to end this marriage. We can work out the details about the kids."

He stopped to see her response. She was looking down at her hands and then looked up.

There were tears in Connie's eyes as she whispered, "When were you going to tell me about Julia and her daughter?"

Surprised that Connie knew, Oscar became enraged.

"Who told you," he bellowed as Connie tried to shush him.

"Oscar, keep your voice down, the children are sleeping."

"Who told you? Lilia? Edna? Who?"

Shaking her head, Connie said, "What difference does it make? I know this has been going on for quite a while if you have a daughter who is almost a year old. Why,

Oscar, did you do this? I don't understand. I tried so hard to be a good wife to you. Yes, I know I am not what you wanted and that I don't cook things perfectly and keep the house the way you want, but why would you do such a thing to me, to the children? I don't understand this, how you could act this way. Did you ever think about your family and what this would do to them? What will happen to us now?"

Connie's softly spoken words halted Oscar; the speech he had prepared in his mind evaporated into thin air.

"Connie, I don't know. Things were not going well between us for a long time. Things just happened. I never intended it to go this way, but the reality is that you and I have not been happy together, so I drifted back to someone who was more familiar and thought like I did. You're right, it shouldn't have happened. But it did, and Connie, I want a divorce. I've meant to tell you this for a while, but the time never seemed right, it worried me how you would take it and how it would all work out."

"I didn't mean to hurt you or the kids. I love them."

Connie noticed he did not include her in his exclamation of love but said nothing. He appeared to be waiting for her to respond to his request for a divorce. *Is this an appropriate time to tell him I am pregnant? Would it make a difference? Probably not. It seems he has already left the children and me. What should I do? One thing I know for sure is that I will not stay in Tucson. I will return to Los Angeles and my family. That would not be easy considering how they disapprove of my children and me, but I have no other options.*

Connie was still upset but felt more composed. At least it was almost all out except the last part. She took a deep breath and looked at Oscar, the man she loved, and said, "Well, Oscar, there is one more thing you should know."

Fear crossed his face as he waited for her to continue. Could there be still more information about Julia that Connie had not yet revealed? "I'm pregnant," she mumbled.

Oscar seemed surprised and realized that this made things even more complicated. "How many months?" he asked.

"The baby will be born in November in Los Angeles. I am not staying here."

"But, Connie, if you move back, I won't be able to see the kids," he said.

"You figure it out, Oscar. I can't deal with this anymore. I have to figure out how to get out of here. You know, I never liked Tucson. I think it is a hot, stinking place lacking any sophistication. I'm glad to be leaving." Hurt by Connie's comments, Oscar let them go. That was not like him because he loved Tucson and was quick to take offense whenever it was maligned. *But we have so many other details to work out. What she thinks of Tucson is not relevant*, he told himself.

"Connie," he said, "I'd like to move out as soon as possible."

Connie was not expecting everything to happen so fast. They had just moved into the Grand Avenue house and now Oscar was moving out. Apparently, that had been his plan all along.

"What do I tell the kids, Oscar?"

"I don't know, Connie. I'll talk to them. I have to figure out what to say. What do you want me to say?"

"How about the truth, Oscar? You've been screwing around with your old girlfriend and want to marry her now."

"Don't be crude, Connie."

"Don't you dare tell me how to act or what to say. You are the one who has caused this marriage to fall apart by your infidelity," Connie said angrily.

"Connie, you have a role in this, too. It is not all me. Yes, I am the one who got someone pregnant, but this is about a marriage that wasn't working either."

"How could it, with you spending money we didn't have and always getting us into debt?"

"I was the one working, Connie. It entitled me to have things I needed for work."

"What did you expect me to do with five little children at home? Work? I told you early in the marriage I did not want lots of children. There will soon be six. How can I work with six children, Oscar? Tell me how. How?"

Exhausted, Connie said, "Go, that's what you want to do. But do not plan on coming back. We are finished, Oscar. I am sorry I ever married you." She climbed into her side of the bed fully clothed turning her back to Oscar. Her heart was breaking, but she could not say another word. Her words meant nothing to him. He was already gone and ready to move on with someone else. She knew that nothing would change his mind.

Oscar sat on the bed for a long while, looking at Connie and thinking over what she had said and wondering to himself how it would work out. He would have to move back to Los Angeles. Julia would not be happy about that, but he had no choice. He had to be near his kids. He wanted to be near them, and he would have to support them since Connie was right; she could not work with so many children to care for and an infant.

Oscar unlocked the door and got into his pajamas. This would be his last night here. It was too late to go tonight, and he was too tired to leave. Tomorrow was soon enough. The kids slept through the ruckus and would learn soon enough that their life would be radically changing and that another move was coming up.

CHAPTER 29

Oscar left for work the next day without saying a word to Connie. She felt defeated and mortified for not knowing what had been going on. There had been signs, but she had been too busy trying to keep up with the kids and house to sit down and think about them, and besides, that was not her way. Connie was not one to dwell on things and try to figure out other people's motives. She lived a more external life.

Besides being pregnant, the shock of Julia's mother calling her and Oscar's declaration of wanting to leave had left her severely depressed. It took all her willpower to drag herself out of bed the next day to get breakfast stuff on the table for the kids. They all came into the kitchen at once making racket and bringing a whirlwind of energy with them into the room. Connie could not stand, so she sat down.

Alarmed, the children all turned to look at her. "What's the matter, Mommy? You don't look too good," they said with fearful eyes.

What do you tell your children, she asked herself? She wished she had a clue what to say. The truth seemed too much for small children and could turn them against their father. She did not want to do that even if she believed Oscar deserved it. She had to say something though since their father would no longer be around. He still had to come and get his stuff. He was moving into Julia's place, wherever that was. She wished she had someone to talk to about all the chaos in her life. In the past, she would have called Lilia, whom she considered a close friend, but now she knew, based on Oscar's anger about who told her, that Lilia and his other sister knew about the "other woman." Everyone knew but her. Even the parish priest. It overwhelmed her with sadness. She needed to pull herself together since the kids were still staring at her, waiting for an answer.

"Can you all gather around me," she asked gently. The children all came to her, waiting for her to say something. She hugged them and looked at their waiting faces.

"Hurry and tell us Mommy," they shouted. "We're hungry."

Just like children. No time to wait. Looking at their tussled hair and messy faces, she said, "Your dad is moving to another house. He will not be living with us anymore." As she uttered the last sentence, Connie had to stifle a sob.

"Why?" they asked. "How come he will not live with us no more? Doesn't he love us anymore?"

"Yes, he loves you all, but he was not happy living with us, so he will live somewhere else."

No need to mention the other child. They did not need that information.

"Also, we will be moving back to Los Angeles. That is where I am from."

"But, mommy, we like it here. We like the mountains behind the house and the tarantulas. We enjoy splashing in the big water puddles. It is fun here. We want to stay here."

"I know but we can't stay. We need to move. It will be two weeks before we go. I must make plans, so you still have time to play in the mountains behind the house." She turned to her eldest daughter and said, "I will be counting on your help a lot more with your dad gone." Turning to her eldest son, she said, "You will now be the man of the house."

Somewhat appeased, the kids asked, "What's for breakfast? We're hungry."

Feeling badly for the children, she said, "Would you like pancakes?"

"Yes! Yes! We want some," they shouted with unconcealed glee.

"Okay, go in the other room and I'll call you when they are ready," Connie said trying to stifle a smile at their exuberance and blissful ignorance of all that was going on around them.

Connie gathered the ingredients, so she did not notice when her eldest daughter had silently slipped out the door. Her daughter went outside and sank down in front of the large palm tree that took up most of the front yard. Ever since moving in, it was one of her favorite places to sit and think. She sat there for a long time with tears streaming down her face. Why would her dad do such a thing, she kept wondering? She loved him and thought he was a good man. Henceforth, in her mind, if a good man would do such a thing, then you could not trust any man. And so, it was on that day the eldest Lopez daughter made a sacred vow to herself that she kept secret for many, many years. She vowed to never marry or have children. And although she was only nine years old, she kept half her vow her entire life.

Connie soon had all the ingredients assembled, and she fried the pancakes in her favorite cast iron pan. It was old and pretty beat up, but it was one she had bought when they were first married, and she loved that memory of a happier time long gone. As the pancakes sizzled, the kids drifted into the kitchen and for a couple of minutes Connie lost track of her troubles and focused on her kids and their delight in having pancakes for breakfast. *Let them enjoy themselves before the upcoming move,* she thought. She still didn't notice her eldest daughter was missing, and that she did not come in for breakfast.

CHAPTER 30

They spent the next couple weeks packing and getting ready for the move to Los Angeles. Connie did not have a place, but her sister Lucille had promised to help her find something and Oscar had been looking, too. Connie was counting on her family's assistance, but she knew it would come at a high price. They still had not forgiven her for marrying Oscar and for having so many children. She explained to the kids they needed to get all their things together and only take the belongings they could not live without. They would not be taking everything with them to their new home.

Moving day arrived and as they loaded the last items into the car, Connie walked around the Grand Avenue house one last time. The house was a complete mess. Empty boxes lay strewn on the floor. Discarded broken toys were thrown in the bedroom corner and the kitchen looked ghastly with paper and plastic bags everywhere and an overflowing trash can. She should do more cleaning. The stove needed scouring. But there was no more time. They would have to leave it this way. It was time to go. This Grand Avenue home had been hers for a short time and she had suffered heartbreak here. She was glad to be leaving this house and Tucson.

Oscar would be driving them to their new home. He had found housing for them in Los Angeles. It would be a long trip with the kids. It was supposed to take seven hours or so but with lots of bathroom stops for the kids and

Connie it took nine hours before they arrived late evening. Everyone was exhausted, including Connie and Oscar. It was hard to see the place in the growing darkness. A series of large tenement buildings stood in front of them. They would have to find their building. Several of the kids were asleep and the youngest child was whimpering he was tired; he wanted to go to sleep and did not want to walk. Connie took a deep breath and opened the car door.

She had to admit the place did not look welcoming. In fact, it looked scary. *Maybe*, she told herself, *it is because it is so dark.* She picked up the youngest in her arms and headed for the buildings. Oscar was gathering the rest of the kids out of the vehicle and grabbed two suitcases. He walked behind her with the kids and luggage. On arriving at the first building, it was clear it was not theirs. It was numbered "5" and their building was Number "2." After a bit of searching, they located their building. Their apartment was on the second floor and you could only access the upper floors through the stairwell. There did not appear to be any elevators in sight, so they headed for the stairs with the children trailing behind.

Oscar walked into the apartment with Connie following holding her youngest in her arms. Distressed as she looked around, she saw a one-bedroom unit with a tiny kitchen, but more alarming was the buzzing sound that could be heard in the room.

"What's that flying around, Mommy?" asked the kids with genuine curiosity.

Connie looked up and saw something she had never seen before: a flying cockroach. It was hideous and made her cringe as she batted one with her one free hand as it moved toward her. The place appeared to be filled with them. The kids ran around trying to catch them. Connie screamed at them to stop.

She looked at Oscar with a look that said, "Why did you do this?"

"Look, Connie, I had no idea the place would be so bad. Let's get the kids settled for the night and we'll plan on finding another place as soon as possible."

Oscar felt bad about leaving Connie and the kids at that place, but they had been on the road for hours and they were all exhausted. It was late, and they had no other options. He would have to find a better place as soon as possible. For the short term, they would have to stay there. He left them with a heavy heart.

He would have to move Julia and their child to Los Angeles, too, so he would look for a place for them tomorrow. Once he got Connie, and the kids settled, he would head back to Tucson for Julia.

Connie looked around dismayed and finally told the kids to get into their pajamas.

"But, what about the bugs, Mommy?" they asked. "What are we going to do to keep them away from us?"

"I don't know. I will buy spray tomorrow but for tonight, pull the sheets over your heads tight. It will be okay. I think they will settle down when we shut off the lights."

150

But Connie was wrong. The bugs came into their own in the dark and flew all around the apartment. Connie wept in her bed with the sheet over her head. She had to cry quietly so the kids would not hear her. She thought she had succeeded, but her eldest daughter heard her. The eldest worried that it was all too much for her mother; this even before she was informed of her mother's pregnancy, for Connie had not yet told the kids.

With daylight the next morning, Connie could get a good look at the place, and what she saw further frightened her. There were mouse droppings by the stove and the buzzing was continual. Oscar had to get them out of here right away. She would call her sister Lucille and see if she would help her find another place. Connie called her sister as early as possible and Lucille agreed to come pick up Connie and the kids. Lucille suggested they look in another area of town near the University of Southern California (USC). She said they might find something there that Connie could afford.

Lucille's car was large enough to accommodate Connie and her five kids. Jostling to get into the car, the kids fought for seats by the window. Annoyed and frowning, Lucille turned around and told the kids to settle down. She also told the kids when they arrived at each location, they would have to duck far down in their seats, so they could not be seen. She explained that landlords did not like to rent to anyone with so many kids. Turning to Connie she mentioned they were headed to an apartment on 24th Street. Lucille cautioned Connie not to even hint that she was pregnant. This caused an immediate hush in the car for those old enough to understand. Connie's secret was now out.

The 24th Street place was respectable compared to their current location. It had two bedrooms, a small kitchen, and a living room. There did not appear to be any bugs in sight. It was small, but Connie could make it work. Connie crossed her fingers as she held her youngest in her arms. She would tell the landlord she had three children. Smiling she saw the landlord waiting by the door. Lucille was strolling behind her. Connie decided to only show him two kids but to tell him there were three. The youngest was in her arms and she had the eldest daughter with her.

The landlord gave Connie an appreciative look. Though pregnant, she still was beautiful. She was only 35 years old. He did not like to rent his places to people with lots of children. They created too much wear and tear on the buildings. He felt the same way about dogs. He did not like them, either. In fact, sometimes they caused more damage than children. He decided he would rent to her though his policy was normally limited to two kids, but she seemed okay, clean, and articulate. She had her sister with her, too, who was also quite a looker. He agreed to the price and told her she could move in next week.

Connie was pleased and relieved. It terrified her that she might not be able find a new home and that they would have to stay longer in that awful place. Lucille gave her a wink as they walked to the car. The kids still had their heads ducked down but could be seen peeking out every so often.

They had better get out of here before the landlord noticed. Lucille rushed to the car and told the kids as she got in, "Stay down, you guys are moving in."

"Yay," the kids shouted pushing each other. The youngest one was now crying.

Lucille looked at Connie and said, "I don't know how you do it. I couldn't do it. More credit to you. They are a handful."

Connie turned and looked in the back seat at her children's eager faces and felt love and relief they would be okay. Now, if she could only get past this pregnancy, she might survive. At this point in her life, she could distinguish her depression and yet there was no one to tell, talk to, or to complain to. Oscar did not care, and the kids were only interested in their own needs. Her family thought she was crazy to have so many children and to be getting divorced with a child on the way. As though all this was her idea. Somehow, with prayers and God's help, she would get through it. Connie was determined but at the moment was not sure she had the inner resources needed.

They moved in and got to know their new neighborhood. It was located in a rough area of Los Angeles, but it would have to do. Connie was now in her seventh month and with her weight gain and swollen ankles, it was getting harder to get around. She was not feeling well and keeping up with the children was getting progressively more difficult.

There was chaos in every room and the dishes continued to pile up in the sink. Her two daughters were in charge of the dishes, but they often fought over whose turn it was to wash them and sometimes neither one followed up, so they remained in the sink. Both girls also had assignments to straighten the house, sweep and dust but like all children were easily distracted and left the tasks undone.

Some days Connie could not function, but she was holding on. Oscar came by once a week to bring food money though it never seemed to be enough. He gave Connie $60 a week to cover groceries and all the children's costs. This was never adequate to even cover the cost for all their shoes, but Connie somehow stretched every dollar to get the maximum benefit. She knew how to watch every penny. Still, by the end of each week, she would have run out of money and would wait patiently until Oscar came by with the weekly allowance before buying any further groceries.

She tried to spring for some treats for the children whenever she could manage to save a couple of dollars. She loved to treat the children to warm glazed donuts after mass on Sunday. Connie appreciated seeing the gleam in their eyes when they took a bite of the freshly made hot donuts.

She had heard Julia was pregnant, too. This angered her but there was nothing she could do.

CHAPTER 31

Connie felt she was at a shattering point as her pregnancy progressed. She alerted Oscar she needed to speak to him alone the next time he came by to drop off the weekly allowance.

"Oscar, I have to take a break."

"What do you mean, a break, Connie? From the kids? What are you saying?"

"I'm saying I have to rest, Oscar. I'm exhausted and can no longer handle the kids. You have to take the kids."

"Are you kidding, Connie?" Oscar asked, exasperated. "Where would I take them? Julia would not allow me to bring them to the house and there is not enough room, anyway."

"You figure it out, Oscar. I have to go."

"But where will you go, Connie? And for how long?" he asked, worried about the new responsibility being cast upon him.

So, they came up with a plan that required Oscar to move into the house and watch the kids. He was to take the kids to nearby Exposition Park and Connie would leave while they were out of the house. The plan suited both adults but did not work so well for the children.

Oscar often took the kids to Exposition Park on outings, so when he came and said they were going out for the day, the kids ran out the door without a backwards glance at their mother. They went there so often they were familiar with all the events and exhibits and knew their way around the park. They spent half a day there and then Oscar took them out to lunch. He thought of telling them at lunch about their mother's leaving but decided he had better stick to the agreed agenda.

On arriving back home, Connie was nowhere in sight.

"Where's Mommy?" the kids asked. Oscar looked around and saw Connie had been true to her word. She had packed her stuff and left. He saw an envelope on the table the same time the two oldest children did. They ran over and picked it up. It was labeled: 'To the Kids.'

"What is it," queried the others. "It looks like a note," said Christina holding the envelope.

"Open it."

Tearing open the envelope, out fell a brief note from Connie. It said:

> Dear Kids,
> I am going away for a while. Your dad
> will take care of you until I return.
> Please mind him.
> Love,
> Mommy

Oscar watched the kid's reactions. The youngest, Larry, cried saying, "I want mommy." The others looked surprised and saddened. This would be difficult, he thought to himself. Julia would not be happy about him leaving her either. He did not know when Connie would be back and contacting her at her mother's house would be impossible.

He looked around and said to the kids, "Let's clean up this joint and then everyone can get their pajamas on."

"But Pop," the kids protested, "It is only 6:30 PM."

"I know, he said, but you can watch television before going to bed."

They all scrambled to their room to get into their pajamas. Only his eldest daughter stood there looking at him.

Finally, she said, "When is she coming back? Is she coming back? I know she has been very, very sad and depressed with all the stuff going on and being pregnant and all." She said all this in a disapproving tone, which was not missed by Oscar, but he decided not to comment on it.

"Look, I really don't know any more than what was in the note. I know she was going to her mother's because she has been sick and managing you guys and being unwell was more than she could handle."

"Really?" said his daughter. "Don't you think you have any blame in this?"

"Hold on," he said. "Do not talk to me like that. I'm your father and I won't have it."

"Yes, you are my father," she spat, "but look at the mess we are in," and she stomped out of the room.

Well! Oscar thought to himself. *This is going to be much more difficult than I expected.* It was then he decided he would run the household like the Army. He was familiar with how that worked, and he was hoping it would work with the kids.

Early the next morning, he marched into each of the bedrooms and yelled, "Up and at 'em! You've got 10 minutes to breakfast."

Stunned, the kids jumped out of bed, not sure what to think. Did their dad think they were in the Army? Stumbling to the one bathroom, they took their turns and rushed into the kitchen. Everyone was there but his eldest daughter.

Oscar turned to Christina and said, "Where is your sister?"

"I don't know. She could be anywhere."

"Go find her," he said. "Tell her she had better get in here."

Oscar had a pan filled with scrambled eggs he was serving when his daughter walked into the room. A sullen expression graced her face.

"Get a plate," he said pointedly to his eldest daughter.

"I don't like eggs," she replied.

"Well, then I guess you will not eat."

Shrugging her shoulders, she grabbed a piece of toast. Everyone else was talking when Oscar said, "I want to tell you about the rules we will have to follow while your mother's gone. Please listen and remember them." Oscar had everyone's attention.

"Look, I don't know how long your mother will be gone, so to make it easier for all of us I have made up rules everyone has to follow. They are simple. It is important everyone do their part and I'm counting on you kids."

"Why do we have to have stupid rules?" asked Michael. "We didn't have rules with our mother."

"Yes," Oscar said, "And look at the mess here. We need to have more order. With so many of you, it is easier if everyone does their part and cleans up after themselves and that includes the dishes. There is always a pile of dishes in the sink and on the kitchen table. That must stop. If you use a dish, you wash it and put it away. Also, I will not be hiding the lunch fruit and other treats. I know your mom did, and you kids found them and ate them, anyway. If you want fruit and cookies in your lunch, then better not eat them before they get into your lunch. Everyone got that?"

Glumly, everyone looked at their dad.

"And," he said, "You must make your bed each day. Just like the Army. It is important to be neat. It makes for a nicer environment."

"Ah, I don't want to make my bed," grumbled Larry. "I don't even know how to make a bed."

"No problem, junior, I'll teach you today," Oscar said gently.

"Do I have to, Dad?"

"Yes, everyone does, including me."

Disgruntled, the kids left for school and the youngest went with Oscar. *Well,* he thought to himself, *that went well. Wonder how dinner will go? Connie had better not be gone too long.* He was not sure he would survive with the kids on his own. He never understood how much organization was needed to manage the kids. No wonder Connie was always complaining she could not get it all done.

Oscar's Army routine worked well in it kept the house more ordered and the sink empty of dishes. The kids complained constantly but mainly to each other, afraid to voice their concerns to their dad. The youngest one pulled the covers over his bed pleading he was too small to get behind the bed to tuck the corners in properly. Oscar overlooked his bed because of his youth but made the others comply.

Meals, too, were done according the Army protocol. Everyone had to be on time once the meal was ready. No dawdling was allowed. If you did not show up on time for meals, you did not eat. Oscar had to admit that with meals, showers, school, and bedtime schedules, there was no time left to rest, much less think. The kids were running him ragged.

For a second, he considered his harshness with Connie and all the criticisms he had heaped upon her for not keeping the house and kids in order. Not one to spend too much time for introspection, he dismissed the thoughts and yet; he had to admit; he had a twinge of guilt over his cruelty.

Julia spent her fury on Oscar whenever he returned home for a brief respite. "Why do you have to take care of Connie's children?" she would scream. Oscar would merely shake his head and say, "They are my children, too, and they need someone to watch them. I am doing what any father would do, Julia, so get off my back."

"What about us here? Your children with me. Don't they need you too, Oscar?" Julia asked sadly.

CHAPTER 32

Connie had resisted going to her mother's house until the last month of her pregnancy, but she was so depressed and sick she could not handle the kids. Her mother had been her only option. She wondered how Oscar was doing. He was always badgering her about the state of the house, the meals, and how the kids looked. *Well, he will have to learn to manage. He will see it was not as easy as he thinks.*

Connie needed to rest and pull herself together. She had been so disheartened and being pregnant only added to the deterioration of her overall state of mind. Connie knew she did not have the luxury of feeling sorry for herself. She was 34 years old, pregnant, about to be divorced, and soon to be a mother of six children. *Oh, God, how would she manage it?* She had no clue. She was also feeling guilty about leaving the kids the way she did, with no goodbye or explanation, just the note on the table.

She needed a shoulder to cry on, or least someone to listen to her problems. That someone, however, would not be her mother. Maria was not the most sympathetic person even in the best of times and, with current circumstances as they were, Connie's mother would be little comfort. Connie knew that when she returned to her mother's home, so she kept her feelings bottled up inside.

She was in her ninth month and was having trouble with the pregnancy. She wished it was over. Being in her mother's house did not add to her well-being, either physically or mentally. She was losing sleep over how Oscar was managing with the kids, not sure he was up to the task, but he had been her only option. As the time for the new baby drew near, Connie was dreading it more. *How would she manage? She could not work with all the kids and a new baby.* She felt so dejected; it made her withdraw further into herself.

Maria loved her daughter and did not know how to help her. She noticed Connie's deepening depression and tried to engage her by offering her different foods. She attempted to cheer her up by distracting her and offering to take Connie shopping to buy new clothes for the baby. Nothing worked. Maria called her daughter Ruthie and asked her to come over and visit with Connie. Maria was hoping a visit might brighten Connie's outlook.

Ruthie was the worst choice since she had little sympathy for Connie's plight. She wasn't too crazy about her children, either. On the way to her mother's house, Ruthie tried to think of something to say or do that might cheer Connie up. Ruthie was a direct person and always felt the best way to handle everything was to hit it head on. She was like Oscar. Still, she wanted her sister to feel healthier and better.

On entering Maria's house, Ruthie called out, "Hi, everyone. I'm here and I brought tamales for lunch. Beer, too." This was the optimum Ruthie could do. She loved her sister but was not much for handholding or offering sympathetic advice. So, when she saw Connie, she uttered the first thoughts that came into her head with little thought or reflection on how they would be taken or perceived.

"Connie," she said, "You have to pull yourself together. You have all those kids to take care of. You have no time for feeling sorry for yourself. I know it is hard, but you wanted to marry Oscar and so here you are soon to be a divorced mother with six kids. It's a tough position to be in. You'll be okay."

Ruthie herself was not sure she believed her own words, but she wanted Connie to improve and felt telling Connie to pull herself together was the best way. She could never understand what Connie saw in Oscar. Yes, he was handsome and maybe had charm, but he had not done right by her by getting her pregnant all the time and now leaving her when she was pregnant. No decent man would do that.

Maria stood in the background, frowning. Ruthie was not helping. She was making it worse. What made her think a visit from Ruthie would help? The problem was she didn't think Lucille would be any better, and Carmen was off somewhere and who knew when she might show up. Also, Maria suspected, she would not be helpful, either.

It amazed Connie to see Ruthie. She had seen little of her family since she had returned to her mother's house. She suspected they were avoiding her because they did not know what to say and felt it was easier not to see her. This made her feel even worse but, as usual, she kept her thoughts to herself. Ruthie seemed in good spirits as she held up the large brown bag above her head that held tamales. Connie could see the corners of the bag were smudged with red chili grease from the tamales.

At least she's brought food and I love tamales! Connie thought. She appreciated Ruthie remembering that and bringing them to cheer her up. Connie surmised her mother had called Ruthie and asked her to come and visit. It didn't matter. Nothing would change the circumstances of her life. She had to come to grips with it. For now, she would have two tamales and maybe even a beer. One beer surely wouldn't hurt her. Warnings about alcohol and pregnancy were still far in the future.

The baby was born on Saturday, November 24, 1956, two days after Thanksgiving. Connie named her Rosa. The kids celebrated the holiday with Oscar while Connie stayed in the hospital with her newest daughter. She called Oscar to tell him he had a daughter. He did not tell the kids that their mother called. He asked her when she thought she might return home. Connie said she did not know. She did not want to go back. She wanted to run away but there was nowhere to run, and she did not have the physical or mental capacity to even come up with a plan. The reality was she would return to her children whom she loved.

Oscar was trying to manage two households, and it was best that Connie did not know that Julia was also seven months pregnant at the same time. Julia would give birth to a son in January 1957, two months after Connie's daughter's birth. This would be Oscar's fourth son, but the first one with Julia. She would have two more sons and two daughters for a total of six children, the same as Connie—three girls and three boys. Julia's children would be born close together (1955, 1957, 1958, 1959, 1961, 1965). Running two households was costly. Having so many children added pressure on Oscar to make more money. It was unclear whether Oscar wanted more than the two children he had when he married Julia, or if it was Julia's wish to have six children so that she would have more children than Connie.

CHAPTER 33

Time spent at Maria's recuperating from the birth of her sixth child gave Connie the essential interval she needed to reflect on her life choices. Despite her depression, she could see beyond the last couple of years. This allowed her to see how far she had come from the wide-eyed young woman whose singular goal was to remain in California. She could finally come to terms with the fact Oscar did not love her despite having given him the children he yearned for; it had not assisted her effort to win his love. It had taken her so long to grasp that there was no winning Oscar over. She had paid a high price for loving Oscar.

He was never hers and would never be hers no matter what she said or had done. This was new knowledge to Connie or maybe it had finally reached a conscious level and she could grasp the enormity of it. Even though it was late to realize this, it now set her free. Yes, she did not have Oscar, but she had her children and they loved her and to her utter amazement, she loved them and how they now completed her in strange and amazing ways that she had never expected or anticipated.

Connie returned home to the children the first week of December, exhausted and still having difficulty coping with care for her newborn daughter. Connie was using all her strength to hold herself together; her new baby did not get her full attention. Connie's second daughter Christina would get up in the middle of the night to feed her baby sister when Connie could not do it. Her newest daughter was a sickly child who cried easily and often. This did not endear her to the other children who grew up in a world that forced each one to fend for themselves. The baby could not fend on her own, so Christina spent much of her time feeding, cuddling, and carrying the newborn around, trying to nurture her as much as possible. Connie merely looked on, grateful someone else was taking full charge of her youngest child.

In fact, Connie had never taken to infants. She preferred older children, those close to adulthood. So, when her children were young, she fed and clothed them but did not expend much physical or verbal attention on them. Conceivably, she had not been given attention as a child herself or perhaps there were too many children on which to focus individual attention. Connie may have not known nor understood the importance of having regular, ongoing physical contact with her children. There would be indications that this lack of attention affected her children, particularly her three boys.

With Oscar returning to Julia and his other family, his Army routine gone, the children returned to their old patterns of not making their beds, not washing their dishes as they used them, and not returning things to their proper place. It did not help that the small apartment on 24th Street was infested with mice. Connie and her kids tried to make the best of it, by ignoring the droppings and trying to not leave any food out on the counters. Things returned to their earlier messy state with the required order put in place by Oscar soon forgotten.

Dirty dishes stacked up in the sink. Connie's two young daughters were reminded to keep the house in order and the sink free of dishes. However, there were always more dishes and piles of clothes and chaos wherever you looked, with so many little hands around the house. It did not appear to bother Connie that much and the girls being children were not interested in the housecleaning or staying on top of their assigned tasks. Connie spent part of the year after her last daughter's birth in deep depression, leaving the children to fend for themselves. The children were growing and becoming more independent. She still cooked and insisted they go to church, but they were not constrained with lots of rules like other households. Each child made up his/her own rules and followed them as he/she saw fit. They all knew that getting into any kind of trouble would mean they had to get themselves out, so they were all very careful on how they conducted themselves, even at a young age.

The housing complex had many neighbors, and everyone knew everyone and kept track of each other's kids. Neighbors tended to be snoopy and interested in everyone's business. Connie kept to herself, not wishing to share information about herself or her children. When queried about her status, she would use a one-word response "divorced," leaving the questioner still curious but understanding further questions were unwelcomed. Neighbors learned to say hello to Connie and her children but not intrude into her privacy.

The upstairs neighbor was an alcoholic and was forever trying to engage Connie in long convoluted conversations, often while intoxicated, as she staggered up the stairs to her apartment. What she said never made sense and Connie came to believe the woman was lonely. Connie would hide when she heard her heavy footsteps on the stairs. The whole family tried to avoid her, but it was hard because her young daughter was friendly with Connie's kids, primarily Daniel. The neighbor would appear at the Lopez's' back door trying to make friendly conversation on the pretext of looking for her daughter.

Connie made several close friends during this time and would try to spend time with them listening to music or going to the movies when she could get away from the kids. She was fond of Peggy, her eldest daughter's best friend's mother. They had a lot in common besides their daughters and would chat and drink coffee. Connie also made other friends but was very selective and limited her friendships. It became easier to leave the children for longer periods as they got older. She felt she needed short breaks just to keep her sanity and to talk to other adults. She put her eldest daughter in charge of the children with directions they were to all mind her. With her mother's authority, the eldest daughter bossed the younger ones around. She set up a play school and grocery store. Sometimes the younger children did not want to play.

Connie saved her quarters for laundry day. There were no facilities in the complex where she lived. Each week Connie gathered the children's dirty laundry in two extra-large bags she placed into metal pull carts that could be pulled to the laundromat six blocks away. The children would march behind her forming a crooked trail as they proceeded down the street trotting towards the laundromat. Washing clothes was an all-day event, not only because of the huge piles of unclean clothes that needed care but because there had to be a sufficient number of machines available for washing and drying to complete the job.

Trying to coordinate the time on the washers and dryers for multiple machines was a nightmare, if there were groups of mothers there, too, trying to do laundry at the same time. Sometimes she left the kids at home with the eldest daughter to avoid having to keep track of the children in the closed environment for so many hours. Doing the weekly laundry was a hard task, but one she had to do.

Besides making sure they had clean clothes Connie worried about the state of her children's souls. The only way to ensure her children's salvation was for them to be raised as Catholics. Connie worried how she would provide Catholic school education for all her children. Making the required tuition payments was a continual challenge. Always resourceful, Connie requested a discount since she had four children attending the same school. The problem was the tuition increased annually and then there were the costs for the uniforms. Uniforms, she kept reminding herself, were cheaper than having to provide different outfits for the kids each day.

She had four children in school and one scheduled to enter the following year. This should be worth an additional discount, she thought. She had to go back and talk to the school principal, a no-nonsense nun, who ran St. Vincent's with an iron hand. Connie needed further reductions in her fees to afford to send all five children to the same school. Hopefully, the principal would understand the hardship the tuition placed on a single mom with six kids. Connie persuaded the hard-nosed nun to reduce the tuition costs, which gave her a little more money for food.

Periodically, the school tested the pupils, sending the results home to the parents. During one testing session, Larry tested in the high IQ range. The school contacted Connie and informed her they wanted to place him in a gifted program because he was more advanced than others in his age group. All she had to do was come in to the school to complete the necessary paperwork.

Despite repeated telephone calls, Connie did not complete the required documentation to have her youngest son take part in the gifted program. It was never clear why Connie would not allow her son to advance to the special curriculum offered. She did, however, tell her son he had a high IQ and then admonished him to "stay out of trouble." He later informed his brothers that having that information resulted in him having less motivation to do well in school rather than more motivation.

Oscar would stop by Connie's once a week to drop off the money for the kids. Connie waited for his visit before she could do any grocery shopping. Sufficient funds to meet all the kids' needs were rare but Connie's frugality and money management skills helped tremendously. With the paltry weekly sum Connie received from her ex-husband, she bought groceries, paid the children's tuition, and bought clothes for them. Fastidiously cutting out coupons from bargain throwaway flyers she scanned weekly, Connie could squeeze out every last penny. It was a tight and stressful time and it distressed her that there never seemed to be enough food for her fast-growing kids. She often ate less, so there would be more food for the kids.

On rare occasions when Oscar was out of town on a job, Julia had to drive over to the house to drop off the weekly money. Connie refused to go out to her car and always sent one of the kids to get the money. Julia handed the envelope over and left but it angered her that Oscar forced her to be in a position of having to deliver money to Connie.

The kids ate everything in sight, and they knew if they showed up late for dinner they would not eat. Food ran out. You needed to be early if you wanted to get your share. Larry hated pinto beans, one of the often-served meals. He always skipped dinner whenever pinto beans were the sole performer.

Connie suspected but did not know for a fact that things were very different at Julia's house. She was sure that there were larger quantities and healthier food in the second home. This made her deride the other woman secretly. Not so much for taking her husband but for taking food out of her kids' mouths, though she never shared this thought with anyone. Julia detested that Oscar had to make weekly trips to Connie's house. It frustrated her even more when he shared his worries that they did not have enough food. She wanted him to concentrate on her children, her house, and her. Though she wouldn't admit it to anyone, she remained jealous of Connie long after she had married Oscar.

During his weekly visits, Oscar would distribute quarters and half dollars to the kids for their allowance. The money always came with authoritative advice such as, "You guys better not get into any trouble or get pregnant because if you do, you will be on your own."

Connie would shrug at Oscar's repeated warnings to her children. Each of the kids took these words to heart knowing their dad meant them. They would always be responsible for whatever happened to them. No one, not their mother or father, would save them or come to bail them out of jail. This knowledge, besides scaring them, kept them on the straight and narrow. That was Oscar's intent, but it made for an insecure childhood. Oddly, it had another consequence. It developed strong independent kids at an early age who took their responsibilities seriously and who never looked to others for rescuing.

Besides dishing out advice to his kids, Oscar sometimes spoke to Connie in a harsh and sometimes insulting manner to such a degree that even he sometimes felt ashamed of himself. *Why am I so mean and belittling to her? Do I still love her? What was up with my behavior? Nah, I wasn't sure I ever loved her, but do I care for her deeply? And on some level, I miss her.* He often asked himself these questions once he left Connie's house. To make matters worse, Oscar had a habit of making these disparaging comments to Connie in front of the children. Rather than arguing or saying something in response, Connie would leave the room. Despite his bad behavior, Connie never responded negatively. In her heart, she nursed bitter thoughts towards Oscar, but she refused to lower herself to his level.

Often angered by her father's comments to her mother, Rosa would ask her mother, "Why don't you say something? Why do you allow him to speak to you like that?" Connie would shrug and turn away without responding.

Despite his injurious behavior, Connie always maintained a cool attitude toward Oscar whenever he came around even when he hinted he wanted to be "friendly." Connie would ask her eldest daughter to stay, "Until your dad leaves." This always made her daughter laugh and she would say to her mother, "You were married to him, you can handle him." Connie would insist she stay, so she did. It is unclear why Connie was so nervous about being alone with Oscar and when pressed why she would say, "You know how your father is," which did not answer her daughter's question. From her perspective, he gave no indication of interest in her mother. At the time her daughter thought it must be an adult thing she did not understand.

Oscar was also known to treat Julia badly on occasions, insulting her and demeaning her in front of her children. He seemed compelled to put down the women around him because of his own insecurities. Did this behavior stem from his need for a mother and the mothering he never had? Most likely, Oscar had no awareness of the deep wound that occurred early in his life, nor was he aware that he had spent his lifetime trying to find the mother he never had. He knew he hated his father for his failure to save his mother and his children. He spoke of it often whenever the subject of fathers came up. But did he know how he took it out on the women and daughters who loved him? That was never clear.

Connie now had more information about what was going on with Oscar and knew that Julia had two children by him before she had officially divorced from him. It seemed, from what she heard from his sister, that Julia was pregnant again. She wondered if Julia knew what she was getting into with Oscar. Anyway, that was not her problem. Her days of having children were over and she was glad.

She was happy she divorced Oscar and then she remembered; he had asked her for the divorce on that dreadful night, not the other way around. She put all such thoughts of that night out of her mind. Better to forget it all. It was too painful to remember. Connie was practiced at ignoring things she did not want to see or address by pretending they didn't exist. Her daughters called it "doing a Chula" since it was a behavior she often engaged in when dealing with the children.

Anyway, Connie thought to herself, *my days of romance and men are over.* Though she was only 36, she felt much older. Connie was still young and attractive despite having had six children. She observed men eying her as she walked down the street and in church, but she pretended not to notice. She wanted nothing to do with them. Her eldest daughter would beg her to consider going out to a movie or out for lunch with any of the men that asked.

Connie would shake her head and say, "You can't trust any of them," refusing to discuss it further. She never went out again nor would she consider the possibility, to the dismay of her daughters who wanted her to be happy and to enjoy her life since she was still a young woman. Connie believed all men were untrustworthy and would betray you until her last days. She warned her daughters to be wary of men and their intentions.

CHAPTER 34

Michael, Connie's eldest son, randomly wandered the neighborhood streets as did his brothers and sisters out of sheer boredom and nothing much else to do. Frequently, he would pass a local liquor store that was approximately three blocks away from his 24th Street home. If he had any leftover loose change from his weekly allowance, he would stop in the store and purchase a candy bar or Saladitos, the salted dry plums the kids craved. One day as he passed by, a man came out of the store, identified himself as the store owner, and casually asked him if he was interested in making money.

Pleased, he responded with an enthusiastic, "Yes!"

"All you have to do," explained the owner, "is manually put up the store awning each day and sweep the floors before the store opens. I'll pay you 75 cents to do it. Do we have an agreement?"

Michael, who preferred to be called Mike, nodded. It was to be the beginning of a long working relationship that lasted many years. It thrilled Mike because he had a job at twelve years of age, his own pocket money and was no longer dependent on the weekly quarters and fifty-cent pieces handed out by his dad. Eventually he was promoted to stocking the shelves, then in charge of inventory control and finally became a sales clerk, all by the time he was fourteen years old.

He was a naturally friendly guy, which made him a first-class sales clerk. Customers liked him. Often customers would say to him, "Hey, you're not old enough to sell or buy liquor. What's the deal here?" He would shrug his shoulders in a non-concerned manner. Customers usually dropped their trepidations as they paid for their purchase and left the store. He told his eldest sister that no one ever reported the store's illegal operations and he continued working there throughout high school, but they did!

Not that Mike didn't do a little experimenting of his own with booze and cigarettes, but it soon lost its appeal. He would later recount that his early exposure to addiction made him determined to never smoke cigarettes or drink. He had seen at a young age what nicotine and alcohol did to people.

His most vivid memory of those early working days is that of customers lingering outside the store before the official opening banging on the front door begging for just one cigarette or drink, saying they could not wait any longer to get in. On occasions, the liquor store owners would allow him to throw one or two single cigarettes out the door just to get the desperate customers to stop their repeated knockings. Laughing, he said, "That always did the trick." No liquor was tossed out the door, however.

His brother Larry had been following the recycled bottle trail since age seven, even though his collecting often resulted in only a couple dollars a day if he was lucky, no matter how much effort spent. A couple of years later, a friend of Larry's told him about a job in the liquor store down the street. He thought it sounded a lot better than walking miles and miles each day to a dusty and remote construction sites gathering redeemable bottles.

The recyclers weren't too crazy about him when they saw him enter their facility with bags filled to the brim with different sizes of bottles and cans, most dirty and dusty. Staff was required to hand sort them because they had to be grouped by size, shape, and material type to verify the money owed him. The idea of a regular job and never collecting another bottle or can again was exhilarating. It might even be the same liquor store where his brother worked.

Larry wasted no time stampeding to the store the next day and speaking to one of the owners. They hired him on the spot. The year was 1964; he was 13 years of age, and they agreed to pay him paid 25 cents an hour. Larry worked 32 hours a week, making $8 a week. He felt rich compared to his bottle-collecting days. An industrious worker, he felt bad when they later fired his friend saying he was not a hard worker. After ten months on the job, they raised his salary to a $1 an hour. His initial tasks included stocking and gofer jobs until he became a sales clerk in the store.

As the owners' confidence in his ability grew, so did his responsibilities. Soon they had him delivering beer kegs to fraternity parties. The store provided liquor to many of the fraternities on the USC campus, which were located near the liquor store. He was way too young to drive, so they had someone else drive him to the fraternities and various locations. He was charged with making sure the beer was delivered and properly set up. Soon he became the store's expert on this part of the business.

Business was booming in the S & A Liquor store and other merchants in the area took notice with envy. Prior to the liquor store getting most of the fraternity concessions, the grocery market on 32nd Street received a share of the fraternity business. With heavy marketing, special discounts, along with other promotional gimmicks, S & A expanded into the university market quickly gaining the majority market share. One disgruntled grocery store owner snooped around and soon learned that besides hiring minors who were selling liquor, there were other irregularities occurring in the store. He called the Bureau of Alcohol and Beverages and reported his concerns.

On the night of the raid, neither of Connie's children were working, just one owner. Everyone in the facility was arrested and taken into custody. The store was closed down. Formal charges were filed against Sandy, the most active owner in the business. The charges were serious enough to warrant jail time. Fortunately, Sandy's father was a business owner who was on good terms with the local judge who would hear Sandy's case. It was rumored that a $33,000 payment was made in exchange for Sandy getting three years' probation and an agreement that required that he'd never work in the liquor business again. He took up a new occupation, meat packing.

Oscar had his moments of guilt, too, when he visited Connie and the kids. They lived in such shabbiness compared to where he, Julia, and the other kids lived. He was not sure what he could do as he couldn't give Connie more money. Oscar had three kids with Julia and one on the way. He still spent more than he earned. Oscar felt that the first family was not getting the best of the situation. He was right. The second family was living in a nicer house, in a nicer neighborhood, but the children were under his constant scrutiny. He knew Connie did miracles with the little money he gave her, but he never told her or acknowledged it.

Julia was satisfied with her life with Oscar. She had her children, her birds and her garden. It was not perfect, but it was what she had yearned for since her earliest days. Oscar had the same no "Spanish" rule at home policy with his second family. The second group of children did not learn to speak or understand Spanish even though their mother was fluent. Julia continued to resent all the attention and time the first family took, but Oscar loved his children and no matter how much Julia nagged him about going there once a week and on the holidays, he continued to do so until all his children were grown. Julia still harbored fears about Connie's influence on Oscar because of the earlier years when she had waited and waited for him.

Oscar ran a very strict household with both families. In many ways, it was traditional in that men and women had set roles that were supposed to be honored and followed. The children were obligated to honor their father and mother above all else, always following their dictates, never contradicting them even if you were not in agreement. Oscar required his children to follow his rules.

Life in the first family differed from life in the second family in that Connie's children were free to do as they pleased. Connie did not subject them to any stringent rules or watch them that closely. They benefited from this upbringing. They were always responsible for themselves, knowing if they got in trouble; it would be up to them to retrieve themselves from it. Also, they were not encouraged or discouraged to follow any traditional roles. This benefited the girls who wanted to be educated, enabling them to follow their dreams. Connie neither encouraged nor discouraged her children's ambitions. She kept her distance and followed a strict "hands off policy." Almost all of Connie's children received a college education and several had advanced degrees, all of which they paid for themselves.

Connie often prayed asking for help from her favorite saints. She felt that a higher power would look out for her and her children. Oscar was always warning the children in the first family that if they got in trouble, they would be on their own. He saw little value in education for the girls in either family. Education was not important for girls because they would marry. Connie's family tried to help her in their own way. Lucille took her on grocery shopping sprees and Carmen invited them over to lunch, making special meals. Carmen would include her mother and brother Tony at these lunches. They provided gifts at

Christmas and clothes for the children, but Connie still felt their quiet disapproval.

Connie was proud of herself considering how difficult life had been so far. The kids were growing and all were healthy and she had survived her darkest days. A couple of the children had asthma, but considering the heavy smog in Los Angeles that was not unusual.

She was still required to visit her mother once a week. She would take the bus to arrive at her mother's house by late afternoon. Sometimes her sisters were there and they would all share a meal. Lucille, who lived with Maria, would sometimes give her a ride home. They asked few questions about the children.

Rosa was growing fast. Christina spent much of her time caring for and watching out for her younger sister's well-being. Once she learned to walk and was getting around the house, it meant she had to be monitored more carefully so as not to hurt herself or get into any messes. She was a lively and curious little girl.

Every two weeks, Lucille would stop by and pick up Connie so she could do her shopping. With her grocery coupons packed in a small white envelope, Connie and Lucille would visit two and sometimes three grocery stores looking for weekly bargains. Depending on the day of the week, these excursions could take several hours. Connie always left the children at home with her eldest daughter in charge while she did the shopping. The children would beg to go because they hoped to get a special goodie, but one look from their Aunt Lucille told them it was better to remain home with their bossy big sister.

On a chilly winter evening while Connie was out grocery shopping with Lucille, a fire broke out in the apartment. Connie's two oldest daughters had gathered around the small portable heater trying to warm themselves as they often did on extra cold days. The old-fashioned heater had large holes on each side of the small appliance that allowed the flames to disperse the heat. Occasionally, flames would spike and spurt out of the holes. As her two daughters stood in front of the heater in their long flannel nightgowns, a flame shot out landing on the edge of her eldest daughter's clothing.

Flames rapidly crept up the edges of her gown. Yolanda screamed and screamed as Christina, terror stricken, threw her to the floor. The rest of the children ran up to assist smothering out the fire the best they could. They succeeded but not before Yolanda suffered second-degree and some third-degree burns on her left legs and arms. Burn stains scarred the floor. The children did not know what to do with their big sister's injury. There was no way to reach their mother and the burns on their sister's legs started blistering. Still, nothing more could be done but wait for their mother's return to tend to their sister. Christina was frightened by the incident but unharmed.

Connie returned home to find crying children, a smoky house, and an injured daughter. All the kids tried to explain at once what happened, how they had put the fire out and how frightened they had been. Connie rushed to her eldest daughter and asked to see her burns on her arms and legs. She could see they were serious burns. She put the only medication she had on her daughter's blistered skin and said they would go to the doctor in the morning. Her daughter said it hurt and Connie could see large blisters forming on her arms and legs. She gave her daughter an aspirin and put her to bed.

She then lugged the three bags she had dropped by the door when she entered the apartment to the kitchen and unloaded the groceries, saying a silent prayer of thanks. It had been quite a night, and she felt relieved that her children managed the crisis without her. It could have been a greater disaster if the fire had spread.

Connie did not feel comfortable staying in the apartment. She wanted to move, and she had been looking around after the incident. Meanwhile, the landlord had asked her to move her family into a vacant apartment while they made repairs to the burned floor. Connie knew she needed to move before they gave her a formal notice.

CHAPTER 35

While at her mother's house the following week, Connie considered asking Lucille to drive her around to locate another apartment. Apartment owners did not want to rent to anyone with so many children, so Connie would need to lie as she had before. The good news was she was not on welfare, which was a real turnoff to many landlords. Connie never considered it no matter how difficult things got for her. She'd manage to with do with less. Connie had her children to think about and being on welfare was not something she would ever consider even though others, including her family, had asked her why not? Shrugging she would say when asked, "It's not for me or my children. I'll manage somehow." Amazingly, through her frugality and careful stewardship, Connie survived all those years despite limited resources, and she even saved a little money.

Getting up her courage, she asked Lucille, "Can you do me a favor and help me find a new place?"

"Will the kids be with you?" asked Lucille pointedly.

Connie understood intuitively that Lucille would prefer that the kids not come along for the ride like they did the last time. Lucille was not crazy about Connie's kids. Then, it seemed no one in Connie's family liked them. Good kids, they did not deserve the bad rap her family had given them. She knew it was way too late to change the family members' minds. Her mother had influenced them, too. She understood why the children hid in the hall closet whenever her mother and sisters visited and why they couldn't be coaxed out until the visitors left. They knew they were not liked, much less loved. Connie's family did not hate her children. They were not happy to see them and did not do well with children especially when there were so many of them at one time. They were too noisy, too rowdy, and ran around too much for Connie's family.

Looking at her sister, Connie said, "I can leave them at home but will have to tell the landlord I have children. I have to decide how many I want to tell him I have. I'll play it by ear when we get there."

"Will you help me out, Lucille?" she asked again. Lucille gave a slight nod of her shoulders indicating a 'yes' and Connie sighed a breath of relief. That would make it so much easier than riding around on buses trying to scope out rental areas. It was time to move. She would tell the children they were moving when she got home even if she had not yet found a place.

A couple of days later they spent a good part of the day driving around neighborhoods near the USC campus looking for posted rent signs. When they spotted one, they would stop and inquire about the apartment. There were not as many signs as Connie had hoped and some places were in poor condition.

After an hour of looking, Connie said, "Let's call it quits for today. I'm tired and I have to get back to the kids."

Lucille agreed, and they headed home.

Within the month, Connie found a new place on 30th Street. It was larger than her last place, but not by much. The kids were excited. There was not much to move as the furniture was not in the best shape. They took the sofa even though the springs were popping out in the back.

Anyway, it was time for a change. Connie felt it was time to move even though that triggered unpleasant memories of her move from Tucson. She did not consider herself depressed and, if asked, she would explain she was merely exhausted. The betrayal, the divorce, and the birth all mixed in her mind to create a defeatist attitude about life and about men. Connie would retain that belief for the rest of her life and would be heard saying her only salvation was her religion and her children.

Though the new location was not that much further from their 24th Street apartment, the 30th Street neighborhood was rougher and in a high crime area known for its numerous fights and robberies. The family settled in, the kids were busy with their own pursuits, and Connie had more free time. Her teen daughters were busy with school and their extracurricular activities.

Her eldest daughter always wanted to borrow Connie's clothing although she owned relatively few clothes. Connie had one good sweater. It was a soft, forest green and her eldest daughter took an immediate liking to it, wearing it often without her mom's knowledge or permission. Connie generously gave up ownership of her one decent sweater to her daughter who was becoming more distant as she grew older.

The new area they lived in was not well lit, and the children had to be careful when walking around the neighborhood at night. Connie and her children used public transportation, so they spent time a great deal of time waiting at bus stations coming from work, to school and to other activities. Crossing the street in their new locality could be dangerous at certain times and it wasn't because of traffic in the neighborhood.

Gangs roamed the streets, often approaching the girls as they waited for the bus. It was at this time that Connie's children learned how to protect themselves and be consciously streetwise. None of her children joined or became gang members even though there were numerous gangs in their neighborhood who challenged the kids if they were in the wrong place at the wrong time.

Connie wanted the children to continue their Catholic education, so the boys attended a Catholic high school, but Larry did not like Cathedral High School, so he transferred to Loyola High, another school he decided he hated. Being a smart and independent kid, he got himself transferred over to the local public high school without his mother's permission or knowledge by completing the paperwork himself. Even at the third high school, he remained a disinterested student, and he continued working at the liquor store after school. Meanwhile, Daniel was working part time at his father's employer's shop, Tri-Way, and Mike continued working at S & A Liquor, each one forging his own path.

The girls attended Bishop Conaty High School. The nuns and rules were exacting, and Connie's eldest daughter returned to her grandmother's house to live because of her proximity to the school. Both girls were fine students, but it distressed the eldest daughter that the school would not let her take part in the college preparatory classes. The nuns told her she would be better off in the commercial track. Her eldest daughter found this insulting and upsetting and interpreted it as a negative reflection on her scholastic abilities. She would spend years and years trying to prove the nuns wrong, but it soured her high school educational experience, which she felt lacked substance. The Catholic high school, the nuns, and her dad all made Connie's eldest daughter more committed to attending college no matter what it took.

Connie continued to be close to her family even though they did not support her children. They loved her and tried to help her in their own way. Her mother had taken in her eldest daughter when things were going badly years back and agreed again to let her live with her again when she was in high school. Maria felt she was helping Connie. Connie felt alone. She had the children but not much else in her life.

CHAPTER 36

With the children growing up, Christina kept gently reminding Connie she needed to find a job. The child support payments would soon end, and it was her only source of income. Worried that she could not find employment at age 48, Connie began looking. She was fearful she would not find anything after so many years of not working and simply being a housewife. In the 1950s, being a housewife had a positive connotation, but by the 1960s it had lost its luster. Many women worried about even listing it as their occupation. Luckily, Connie found a job at the local five-and-dime store, J. J. Newberry's. Though shy, Connie enjoyed talking and helping others, so this was the perfect job for her. It did not pay well, but Connie was so well trained in the art of frugality she did well on her small salary even though she still had three children at home. She worked there for 17 years until she retired at age 65.

Connie never learned to drive always saying she did not want to learn. She knew the L.A. transit system well, including the ins and outs of transferring. Her new job required that she walk two blocks to catch her bus coming from work. Though not a long distance, it wasn't so bad during Daylight Savings Time but as the season switched back to Standard Daylight Time, Connie became anxious and cautious. Taking every precaution possible, she made it a rule to never have much money on her, only money for bus fare. Taking no purse, Connie kept a small coin purse in her coat pocket which she clutched as she walked down the dark streets after exiting the bus.

Despite her safeguards, Connie was robbed on two occasions on her way home from work. She never lost much money because she had so little on her, and she was never hurt but these night-time events traumatized her and made her more fearful at night.

Connie's new employment also gave her a chance to spruce up her wardrobe. She loved bright colorful blouses and jewelry and was able to indulge in items for herself without worrying about food or clothing for the kids. She could now spend money on things to enhance her life because she enjoyed looking pretty, hence her nickname "Chula."

Going to work caused momentous changes at home, too. Connie took Rosa aside and informed her she would now have to cook for her three brothers. Other than advising her daughter she would have to cook, Connie provided no additional direction. Her daughter said the first couple of meals were complete disasters and that her brothers gave her a hard time as they threw away her prepared dinners. A fast learner, she soon became an excellent cook. Connie was relieved that she no longer had to cook. She had never enjoyed it and now the need to provide meals for her children was over.

With the ending of their high school years, most of Connie's children were thinking of moving on. The first to leave was Christina who moved out at age 19 to attend college. To save money on housing and facilitate her educational plan, she moved in with her boyfriend. This upset Connie. She would call her daughter weeping telling her she was living in sin. To end the repeated calls from her mother about the state of her soul, her daughter married at age 20. Soon thereafter, her youngest son, Larry, left to marry at age 19. Her youngest daughter, Rosa, too, would leave at age 19.

Her eldest daughter, on whom she depended for financial and emotional support, moved to Northern California when she was 21 as she attempted to distance herself further from her mother whom she had supported for many years. Eventually, Connie only had two sons living at home with her. With all these changes, she was finding more freedom from the everyday tasks of keeping house for her children after so many years.

When Connie reflected on the changes in her life, she became nostalgic despite the hard years that had not been easy nor that good. She loved her children more as they grew into adulthood and became more self-sufficient. She regretted that the Catholic education she struggled so hard to provide did not seem to follow them into their adult lives. In fact, they all rejected the basic premises of Catholicism and did not attend church or seem to follow any of the dictates of the Church. This saddened Connie and she would later nag those with children to get them baptized and insisted they make their first communion.

In her older age, Connie was more sanguine, but she continued to worry about her children's souls and lamented to her eldest daughter that none of her children would go to communion at her funeral.

As it turned out, communion services were not allowed in the chapel where her services were held. So, the issue of who went to communion was not up for view here on earth or from Connie's end in heaven. Hopefully, Connie was relieved as she looked down on her children. Though not religious, her children believed in Connie's strong faith and her ability to pray successfully for desired outcomes. In times of crisis, they all called their mother and asked for her prayers for their particular cause. They believed her prayers got results, and this reinforced Connie's faith and connected her to them through religion though more tenuously than she liked.

When Mike moved out at age 25, she felt free to look for a place of her own. Euphoric she would be on her own for the first time in almost 35 years, Connie could not wait and yet she felt somewhat lost. Yes, she had her job but all those years of always having to be responsible for someone and having something to do had filled up lots of time. Now she had time, lots of time. Through the years, she had not had time to make lasting friendships or develop hobbies. *What will I do? Will I get lonely without another soul in the house?* Thinking about it, she told herself one important thing—she would have more time to attend church and special novenas, things she enjoyed and that were more dear to her heart.

Her mother had passed away five years earlier, so she no longer had to make the required weekly visiting trips. At the time of her mother's death, a riff had arisen over money left in her estate. Connie believed that since she was the neediest and since all her other siblings were in better financially circumstances than she, perhaps she could receive a larger share of the small estate. When she asked her sisters and brothers if they would agree to a different distribution, they all declined, which saddened her but did not surprise her.

What angered and caused the family fracture was when her siblings told that it would go against Maria's implied wish, which was if Connie got additional money, she would give it to her children, so it was better not to give it to her. Even in death, the legacy of her mother's feelings about Oscar's children continued. This hurt Connie, so she limited contact with two of her sisters and stopped having any contact with Carmen because of the quarrel over her mother's will. Her two sisters soon passed away, leaving Carmen as her only surviving relative. Her brothers had all passed years earlier.

In her later years, Connie tried to reconcile with her sister Carmen by sending her birthday and other special occasion cards. She hoped for some acknowledgment but never received a response. She never heard or spoke to Carmen again. Connie got her small share of the inheritance, which she saved for her children just as her mother had feared.

Christina moved to the Bay Area, joining her sister Yolanda who had relocated many years earlier. With both daughters in Northern California, they started a campaign to convince their mother to move nearer to them. They wanted to watch over and care for her in her senior years. They asked her to consider moving to Northern California to be closer to them. Declining, Connie would relay she was happy in Los Angeles and wanted to stay there. Mike still worked at S & W Liquor and stopped on his way home from work on Fridays to take his mom out to dinner where they enjoyed and shared camaraderie. Connie liked spending time with her son, and they continued this routine for several years.

Connie adjusted to her new lifestyle getting into a rhythm of working and enjoying time alone without children. After a while, it would be Rosa, her youngest daughter, who would pick her up and take her to weekly dinners until she, too, moved to Northern California. Connie had relative peace in her life now but was still bitter about what had occurred years earlier with Oscar and in sad moments recalled those fateful days, and then she would dismiss those thoughts and remember she was now free and happy to do as she pleased.

CHAPTER 37

As Connie neared her 65th birthday, she decided it was time to retire. Connie resolved to move to Northern California to be near her three daughters. Yolanda looked for a suitable location and found an excellent senior housing in an area of Oakland called Piedmont. There was only one catch. No one-bedroom apartments were available and if Connie wanted one, she would have to be wait-listed.

The location had many great advantages—a nearby Catholic church, a post office, restaurants, and good transportation—that placing Connie's name on the wait list was an easy decision. Her daughters crossed their fingers longing for an early entry date. It took nine months for the one bedroom to become available as there were only three one-bedrooms in the entire five-story senior housing building.

Her three daughters would now have their mother nearby after years of physical separation. The apartment had a tiny kitchen, a living room, and a bathroom and it was located on the second floor at the end of a long hallway which meant less noise from adjacent residences. It even had an elevator if Connie did not wish to climb the stairs. With affordable rent and the added attraction of having laundry facilities on the premises, Connie could not wait to move in. Her daughters made plans to furnish their mother's new apartment, buying new towels, a rug, colorful pillows and a sofa for her living room.

Connie had mixed feelings about starting her new life in Northern California. She had been in Los Angeles for most of her life except those years in Tucson and her two sons still lived in the area. She had postponed moving North for so long with many excuses. Connie wanted to be closer to her three daughters but was scared to leave the familiar behind. Most moves in Connie's life had been traumatic, so she looked upon this one with trepidation. She kept reminding herself, this would be a happy move, reflecting a buoyant time in her life. She wanted to find happiness up north with her daughters and their children.

One reservation Connie had was that she didn't like high steep hills. They terrified her; even the thought of them panicked her. She had heard there were lots of high hills in San Francisco where her eldest daughter had lived originally. Her daughters assured her she would live in a flat area with no hills. Oakland, they told her differed from San Francisco. Unbeknownst to her daughters, it turned out this was not totally true.

Blocks behind Connie's complex were a series of steep hills. After settling in her new place, Connie discovered the hills that weren't supposed to exist. Those inclines called out to Connie. In the beginning, Connie's goal was to cover as many routes as she could from her apartment. This tied in with Connie's desire to test herself and to get more exercise. She began by walking up and down the hills surrounding her Piedmont neighborhood. And walk she did, for miles and miles each day. Connie enjoyed her jaunts and partially overcame her fear of high hills.

The walks strengthened her body and mind. But what astounded her the most was how much she relished walking through the surrounding neighborhood. She would often recount her wanderings and adventures to her daughters. Walking the Piedmont hills became her preferred outing, and Connie had never liked exercise before.

Having Leo's Catholic Church nearby as well as the post office, restaurants and a grocery store added to Connie's contentment. She could walk there easily and to the many shops in her new neighborhood. It delighted Connie to learn that weekly bingo games were held in her new complex and that valuable prizes such as food and toilet paper were awarded. The center scheduled trips to casinos, grocery stores, and other points of interest. Connie took several trips but was not keen on the group tours. Instead, she preferred spending time with others socializing in the community center. She enjoyed drawing and painting, crossword puzzles, and Sudoku.

The move had been good for Connie as she seemed happier than she had been in a long while. Her children saw it and worked on changing her diet to a more healthful one by increasing her fruits and fiber. Connie remained healthy and enjoyed her well-being until her death at age 94, just short by a couple months of her 95th birthday.

Connie also enjoyed casinos though she was never a big gambler. Her frugality prevented her from spending too much money. She stated she wanted to win big to "leave money for her children." Though she loved the slot machines and often went with her daughters for birthday celebrations, Connie did not believe in wasting money. Connie often won tiny amounts of money, which pleased her immeasurably. This was amazing considering she was only playing the penny or nickel slot machines. Sometimes she would go all out and play the dime slot machines. Playing the quarter machines was more than Connie could stand. Too much money could be lost. Like many seniors, the promise of a big win was something that gave her hope. Her daughters wanted her to win since it brought her so much pleasure.

Her eldest daughter had one concern about her mother's new living arrangement. With only elderly and challenged tenants living in the housing complex, she worried that people would be dying all the time, and it would be depressing for her mother to lose neighbors and friends. She was right and wrong. Connie remained a resident for 30 years. Many people died while she lived there and it did not seem to bother Connie. She would mention casually a tenant's passing to her children or that the ambulances had been to the facility to pick up a resident. She did not dwell on it and made new friends there.

Ironically, what bothered Connie was that the senior community celebrated the tenants' birthdays each month. Connie was very secretive about her birthday and her age. The staff knew the birthdates of the tenants because they were part of the application process. Birthdays were posted in the lounge area showing only the day of the month, not the celebrants' year of birth. For many tenants, age was a source of pride. Not for Connie. It angered her, and she would say it was nobody's business how old she was. Her daughters told her she should be proud of her age, not ashamed of it. She often missed the monthly birthday events when it was her birthday month. She did not want to tell anyone how old she was.

Connie loved to tell the other tenants how many children she had and was often found bragging about the number and individual children. This impressed the tenants and gave Connie a deep sense of pride and accomplishment.

Ten years after settling in Northern California, she told Yolanda it was time to make her funeral arrangements. She did not want her children to pay for her death expenses. Soon thereafter, Connie and her daughter visited the Neptune Society to set up a plan for her cremation at her death. When asked where she wanted her ashes spread, she said she did not care. However, as the years went by, she told Christina she would like to be in a location where her children could visit her. Her two daughters and Daniel purchased a niche in a crematorium in Piedmont near Connie's apartment. They would later place Connie's ashes there for the family to visit.

Through the years, Connie had no contact with Oscar after child support payments ended but she heard about him from the children who visited him and talked to him by phone. He remained in Los Angeles moving briefly to Marana, Arizona when he bought a small ranch. He remained there for a short period, returning to Los Angeles exclaiming it was too hot to live in Arizona.

Julia and Oscar raised six children. Like all families, they had good and rough times. Their marriage had tumultuous periods. At one point, Oscar moved out of the house when he met a new love. That relationship changed Oscar. His new love began contacting Connie's six children by writing and visiting them. For some unforeseen reason, she wanted to convince Connie's children, all grown, that she was good for Oscar.

She was the opposite of Julia in many ways. Younger, blonde, adventurous, she convinced Oscar to try new things like rock climbing, golf, and traveling. The new woman made a concerted effort to contact the first family, visiting three of the children. Those who met her said Oscar appeared more outgoing and happier than they had ever seen him.

Several children received letters from Oscar's new love. Yolanda received an eight-page letter from a woman identifying herself as her father's girlfriend. The letters seemed to be asking for permission to continue the relationship and explained the many adventures and activities they were engaging in. Not happy to be receiving letters from her dad's paramour and learning about his personal business in such a strange way, Yolanda immediately contacted her father and asked him to restrain his girlfriend from contacting her siblings or her. She expressed severe distress in becoming involved in his personal business. She wondered about Julia, too, but did not ask her dad. The letters, which had been asking for a response, stopped. She later heard Oscar ended the relationship after a year and returned to Julia. Connie's children never heard from her again.

On March 17, 2002, Oscar passed away at age 80. Julia had already preceded him years earlier. The funeral was held at St. Augustine's Church in Tucson, Arizona. Eleven of Oscar's children attended, as did many other family members and friends. His six sons served as pallbearers. This would be the first time all the children were together. They had all met at one family gathering or another but had not been all together at one time. Several spoke about their dad, including the two eldest daughters from each family. Several of the twelve children had fractured relationships with Oscar during his life, yet they attended his funeral except his youngest daughter by Connie.

When Connie was informed of Oscar's death, she immediately telephoned Rosa to inform her of her father's passing.

As her youngest daughter said, "Hello," Connie bellowed, "Your dad is dead," and hung up leaving her daughter shaken and unhappy about receiving this news in such disconnected and abrupt manner. The father she had really never known was now gone.

Oscar Ward Lopez's obituary listed eleven children, failing to list his youngest daughter by Connie. Years later when challenged about the missing information, a family member from the first family would say there had been a debate about whether to include this last child or not. Apparently, Julia was never told of this child who was born while Oscar was still married to Connie. The family continued to protect this information even after her death.

News of Oscar's passing triggered old memories for Connie. She remembered the early days of their marriage when she believed it would work out. *What a naive girl I had been*, she thought. Through the years, she tried to remember Oscar bitterly, how he had betrayed her, but with foresight behind her, she knew in her heart it was complicated. Through the years, Connie had told her kids their dad was not a good man, but like all things in life, that was not the whole narrative. She had a role in their story and though she hated her tale; she knew she had loved and trusted him early in the marriage.

Her mother's intense dislike and criticism had not helped and added to the drama through the years. *Was it better to have loved and lost like they said, or should she have let him go from the beginning?* She would never know the answer. In old age, Connie had reconciled her early decision to marry.

Soon after Oscar's death, Connie discovered she was eligible to receive his Social Security payment, which was substantially higher than the one she received. She told her daughters she planned on declining the payments because she did not want anything from Oscar. Her daughters made such a fuss that she agreed to accept the payments, which added to her small monthly income and gave her more money to live comfortably.

Connie continued to be concerned for her children's welfare. She worried about them and prayed for them. She continued saving her money, not wishing to spend any of it on clothes or items that would make her life easier. When asked where her nice towels were, she would say she was saving the "good towels" for guests, to the dismay of her children.

Her children explained she had enough money to buy things for herself but after so many years of self-deprivation it was a deeply engrained habit and was not one she wished to break or halt. She and her daughter often got into arguments about the purse she wore when she went out. It was old, beat up and had seen better days long ago, yet Connie insisted on using it. Her daughters and sons bought her new purses. They could be found neatly stacked in her bedroom closet, often with the original tags on them. Connie would discard her timeworn purse only after many years of use and at her daughter's insistence.

Even in later years, Connie still did not care to cook. Her daughters would take her shopping for groceries and they would argue over purchasing certain items. Connie did not want to buy items she thought were too highly priced even though she could afford it. She would take them out of the cart and put them back. This angered her daughters since they were the ones paying for the groceries, but Connie did not want her daughters to spend their money, either. The time came when it was easier for her daughters to do the shopping without their mother, so they did not have to fight over purchasing an avocado that cost over a dollar.

CHAPTER 38

Connie's health excelled well into her 90s and it was only then that her mobility slowed her down. Her children purchased a walker for her house and for when she traveled down the street to church and to do errands. Friends often called Yolanda, laughing while describing "Connie sightings" as she sped down Piedmont Avenue in her walker. Thankfully, despite several falls, she never hurt herself. Connie had made it clear that she wanted to stay in her apartment though her daughters thought she would be better cared for in an assisted living facility.

To honor her wishes, they had someone come in for four hours a day to assist with the cooking, medical appointments, and to cover any needed errands. Connie liked the idea because again, she could stay in her apartment, and she could give up serious cooking. She still had to prepare her breakfast. Her new assistant, Teresa, made lunch and dinner. This did not stop Connie from complaining about Teresa's meals and confiding to her daughter that the assistant's food was just not as good as her own or that of her daughters'. This made her daughters laugh.

Connie still loved to eat out. Her daughters took her out often. Yolanda took her out for meals at her favorite restaurants on Piedmont Avenue. She often complained that the portions served were too large and yet her daughter observed that Connie always finished all the food on her plate. Yolanda started over-ordering, so Connie would have leftovers to take home. This did not please Connie, who saw it as wasting money on extra food, but Yolanda continued the practice and Connie would happily take the remains home for later consumption.

With her mobility limited and extended hearing loss, which Connie denied, her interests began to decline. She no longer wanted to attend mass saying, "The priest mumbled too much," so Yolanda sat Connie in the front row near the altar, hoping the priest's use of a microphone would assist her in hearing the mass. Connie insisted she still couldn't hear the mass and there was no point going any longer. Yolanda had to agree; the priest did mumble despite using a microphone. So, the weekly church visits stopped.

Connie had a favorite big easy chair in her apartment. She covered it with different blankets and towels to keep it clean. Her overstuffed chair saw lots of wear and tear as she watched her favorite television programs, said her daily prayers, and sometimes even dozed there. Connie would rebuff claims she slept in the chair and would become irritated with her daughters when they pointed out she did indeed sleep in the chair.

As Connie's mobility continued to decline, she would fall more and more from her easy chair directly onto the carpeted floor. She could not get back into the chair without assistance. Sometimes, she could contact a friendly neighbor in her building who would come and help lift her back onto her chair. Other times the fire department and

EMT had to be called. Though she had frequent falls they did not result in injuries.

Calls to the fire department resulted in several trips to the hospital for evaluation. Those trips presented problems because both fire and EMT staff wanted Connie to go to Highland Hospital's Trauma Center. EMT staff and Yolanda would struggle to get her sent to Alta Bates Hospital, which was closer and had a less intimidating atmosphere, but had no trauma center. Connie's hearing loss created problems for the first responders. Since Connie did not admit to being hard of hearing, when the emergency staff asked her questions to determine her mental acuity, she would try to guess what they asked and then respond based on her conjecture. Often the questions and her responses did not match. This caused EMT staff to believe she had dementia problems and made them even more insistent that she go to Highland Hospital.

Yolanda would explain her mother was hard of hearing and request that they ask the questions loudly, but they typically ignored her requests. It was only when they got to the hospital and her daughter explained to the intake staff there about the hearing issue that Connie could answer the questions correctly. Fire and EMT staff were long gone by then and the original intake report was left uncorrected.

Connie wore a medical alert necklace that came with a monitor box with an intercom system. She kept it on top of the television in the living room. For service, she had to push the button and monitoring staff would speak to her directly asking if she needed assistance. If she failed to respond to their queries, they would alert the fire department and EMT who would rush to her apartment.

Teresa would come by each morning, letting herself in with a key. Often, Yolanda would stop by on her way to work to drop off food or to check on her mom. Yolanda had a key to the front door entrance, but had given her apartment door key to Teresa, so she could enter without disturbing Connie. Building management had strict rules about providing additional keys. They could not be copied, so her daughter no longer had an entry key to the apartment.

On one occasion, the medical alert monitor box fell behind the television onto the floor. Connie was unaware it had fallen since she paid no any attention to the box. The monitoring staff via the microphone asked Connie if she was okay when the button become engaged during the fall. Teresa was at her apartment that day and when she came in, she heard chattering. Though she, too, was hard of hearing, she could hear the incessant talking in the background.

"Connie, who is that that keeps talking?" she asked perplexed.

Connie said, "I don't know, but they won't stop. They keep talking and talking."

This caused Teresa to search the apartment to determine where the voices were coming from. It was then she discovered the fallen monitor. But it was too late. The fire department was now banging on the door. Teresa opened the door and explained that it was all a mistake.

Early on the morning of March 18, 2016, Yolanda entered the building with a bag full of groceries and knocked on her mom's apartment door. There was no response, so she knocked harder knowing of her mom's hearing impairment. Still no answer. A growing sense of dread overwhelmed her as she tried to figure out another way to get into the apartment.

Using her cell phone, she tried calling her mother's telephone. Standing outside her mother's closed door, she could hear the phone ringing and ringing. Still no response. Panicked, she had no way to enter the apartment as there was no on-site manager. She knew Teresa was on her way, so she headed to work but kept dialing her mother's number. Again and again, there still was no answer. Yolanda had been at work a short time when she got a call from Teresa who advised her that both the fire department and EMT were there. She had called them.

According to the assistant, Connie had gotten up in the middle of the night to go to the bathroom and had fallen. She was conscious but upset when found. She had been on the floor all night. Fortunately, despite taking a heavy fall in the bathroom, she had hit no fixtures, so she had no cuts or broken bones. She was banged up, bruised, and had torn the blue shower curtain off the rail as she grabbed it attempting to break her fall. She had not pushed her medical alert button when she fell; it was on her backside and she could not reach it to activate it.

EMT was taking her out on a stretcher when Yolanda arrived and tried unsuccessfully to get them to take her to Alta Bates Hospital, but even after forcing staff to call their manager; they took her to the Trauma Center at Highland Hospital.

Connie remained at the hospital for hours as they ran test after test on her heart even though her daughter explained it was a mobility issue, not a heart issue. Hospital staff could see Connie was traumatized by the fall but not hurt, but they refused to discharge her. They kept performing more and more heart tests. Her daughter argued with administration and doctors in the unit for her dismissal. Six hours after having arrived at the hospital, the manager in the emergency unit agreed to release her but then it was too late because Christina had taken her mother's walker believing her mother would be not be released. So, Connie was kept in the hospital overnight for observation. She was released the following day and went to spend some recuperation time at Christina's house.

Though not seriously injured, Connie appeared to be severely disturbed by her fall. When Christina asked her mother what had happened, Connie said she gotten up to go to the bathroom and had fallen. She did not know what to do since she could not get up. According to Connie she floated up to the bathroom ceiling and remained there afraid to come down. She began praying when a man appeared. He held her hand and remained with her for hours. She lost track of time. At one point she heard loud knocking on the door and then banging and her phone started ringing. She knew her eldest daughter had come to the door and that she would keep knocking and ringing her phone. Connie said she asked the man to answer the phone or the door because her daughter would not be happy that no one answered. Connie said he would not answer the door or phone even after her repeated pleas. When EMT staff came to her rescue, she said the man disappeared.

When Christina probed further asking her why she had held on all night after having told her more than once she was tired, and wanted to go home, Connie replied, "I was on the ceiling and I had to come down or my children would not know where to find me. I was very afraid but had to hold on. My children had to know where I was."

Connie's daughters surmised their mother left her physical body that night and that the experience so traumatized her that even after her rescue she kept reenacting it by trying to crawl down from the ceiling. Her family requested drugs to settle her nerves, but the drugs did not appear to ease her fears. Her children kept assuring her she was down from the ceiling and safely in bed and that there was no need to be fearful, but it was all to no avail. Connie kept reliving the scene and her body would automatically start to move, both her arms grabbing the edge of the sheet and her legs would start walking.

Although Connie recuperated from the fall physically, she no longer left her bed or walked again for fear of a recurrence of what had happened that fateful night. Connie never recovered mentally, and she continued to have post-traumatic stress disorder (PTSD) events until her death.

While at Christina's house, Connie had a choking incident and had to be taken back to a hospital in San Jose. During that hospitalization doctors determined that Connie's swallowing ability was severely hampered. They advised the family she could easily choke because of this impediment. When asked what they could do, they were advised that she could be fed through a tube in her stomach or she could be fed with the possibility of her choking since her swallowing function was severely impaired. Connie had always stated she wanted no extraordinary intervention as her health declined, so the tube in her stomach did not seem to be a viable option.

Christina and Yolanda debated both options. Neither was good. When doctors were asked, how long would she live if she was not fed, the family was told one to two weeks. The family decided on the latter option, but it was a heartbreaking decision and they were not sure what else to do.

Connie had to be transferred to full care facility as she could not leave her bed and now would not be able to eat. Before transferring their mother, the family explained the eating problem informing the facility she could only have liquids. Days after being relocated there both daughters received an urgent call from the facility saying that they were going to feed Connie. Christina and Yolanda requested a meeting with the entire medical staff to discuss their mother's condition and to clarify directions concerning Connie's care. The meeting was contentious, but the doctors agreed to let Connie stay if she was fed liquids. Her daughters readily agreed to comply. Using a straw, both daughters fed their mother root beer and other liquids but no food for her remaining days.

CHAPTER 39

Now that the food issue was resolved, Connie was made comfortable in the new facility. Though surrounded by family at all times, she slept much of the time. Her post traumatic stress disorder (PTSD) episodes continued even though she was medicated to control them. She lived for three weeks. Her two daughters were with her every day, as was her son-in-law. Her sons made trips from Los Angeles and Las Vegas to visit her and to say their goodbyes. She still recognized her children and her granddaughter, great grandson and her grandson who visited her.

Late in the afternoon of April 28, 2016, Connie slowly passed away surrounded by her two daughters who held her hand. As she had requested, Connie was cremated, and her ashes were sent to Chapel of the Chimes where they would be interred in her niche. Saddened by their mom's passing, they were relieved that she would no longer suffer. She had a long life and she had told them, "I want to go," many times in the recent past.

Now their mother's saga belonged to them. It was, after all, a love story—a journey taken with all of its joy, pain, betrayal, faith and redemption—and now Connie's untold story could finally be revealed to all of her children.

**Connie Lopez
with her daughter Yolanda**

**Oscar Lopez
with his daughter Yolanda**

ACKNOWLEDGMENTS

I want to extend a warm and loving thanks to all my brothers and sisters in my immediate family who were badgered repeatedly to recall incidents and specific events that occurred nearly thirty and sometimes fifty years back in time. I relied on their anecdotal recollections as well as my own research and that of my youngest sister, whose assistance proved invaluable as I worked on this project.

Also, kudos to the Pinole Writer's Workshop who provided insight as the book progressed. Their comments and ideas added depth to my story and made me reconsider the events in Connie's life.

I want to add a heartfelt acknowledgment to my sister Olga from the second family whose goal was always to create a family tree and history for all Oscar's children. She passed away unexpectedly in 2014 and did not live to see this story published.

Finally, I want to heap praise and thanks upon Kimberly Starbuck, John Starbuck and Victoria Chak, who did the initial review of the book. I realize it was challenging work, so their thoughts, ideas and honest comments were truly appreciated.

I have nothing but accolades for Karen Mireau, my editor and publisher, as she guided me through the last steps in completing my book.

Author
Yolanda Lopez

ABOUT THE AUTHOR

Yolanda Lopez grew up near the University of Southern California in Los Angeles. An avid reader by age nine, she became devoted to the written word despite lack of encouragement at home.

She has an undergraduate degree from U.C. Berkeley in Sociology and a Juris Doctor degree from U.C. Davis. She pursued a thirty-year career as a Personnel Director for local city government.

A long-time Northern California Bay Area resident, Yolanda is now retired. She enjoys spending time with her daughter and eight-year-old grandson.

Yolanda's passion for reading and writing has remained. Her story, *Fuimos A Cuba*, recounts details of her detainment in Cuba and other adventures during her trip in 1999. She is currently working on her personal memoir.

Loving Oscar, the story of her mother's life, is her first publication.

Contact the Publisher:
Azalea.Art.Press@gmail.com

Contact the Author:
Email | yolandalopezauthor@gmail.com
Facebook | Yolanda Lopez
Twitter | @YolandaI_Lopez
Instagram | Yolanda_i_Lopez
Blog | www.wordswisdomandwonder.com

Order Books:
Lulu.com
Amazon.com
BarnesandNoble.com

www.ingramcontent.com/pod-product-compliance
Lightning Source LLC
Chambersburg PA
CBHW030714110426
42739CB00029B/153

* 9 7 8 1 9 4 3 4 7 1 3 9 3 *